LEADING
FROM THE
SECOND
CHAIR

Serving Your Church, Fulfilling Your Role, and Realizing Your Dreams

Mike Bonem and Roger Patterson

FOREWORD BY GREG L. HAWKINS

A LEADERSHIP ❖ NETWORK PUBLICATION

JOSSEY-BASS
A Wiley Imprint
www.josseybass.com

To our wives,
Bonnie and Julee,
who have loved us as we are and have believed
in our dreams

Published by Jossey-Bass
A Wiley Imprint
989 Market Street, San Francisco, CA 94103–1741   www.josseybass.com

Jossey-Bass books and products are available through most bookstores. To contact Jossey-Bass directly call our Customer Care Department within the U.S. at 800–956–7739, outside the U.S. at 317–572–3986, or fax 317–572–4002.

Jossey-Bass also publishes its books in a variety of electronic formats. Some content that appears in print may not be available in electronic books.

Library of Congress Cataloging-in-Publication Data

Bonem, Mike, date.
  Leading from the second chair: serving your church, fulfilling your role, and realizing your dreams / Mike Bonem and Roger Patterson; foreword by Greg L. Hawkins.—1st ed.
    p. cm.
    Includes bibliographical references and index.
    ISBN-13: 978–0–7879–7739–9 (alk. paper)
    ISBN-10: 0–7879–7739–X (alk. paper)
  1. Christian leadership. 2. Leadership—Religious aspects—Christianity. I. Patterson, Roger, date. II. Title.
    BV652.1.B67 2005
    253—dc22   2005013526

Printed in the United States of America
FIRST EDITION
HB Printing   10 9 8 7 6 5

LEADERSHIP NETWORK TITLES

Leading from the Second Chair: Serving Your Church, Fulfilling Your Role, and Realizing Your Dreams, by Mike Bonem and Roger Patterson

The Way of Jesus: A Journey of Freedom for Pilgrims and Wanderers, by Jonathan S. Campbell with Jennifer Campbell

Leading the Team-Based Church: How Pastors and Church Staffs Can Grow Together into a Powerful Fellowship of Leaders, by George Cladis

Organic Church: Growing Faith Where Life Happens, by Neil Cole

Leading Congregational Change Workbook, by James H. Furr, Mike Bonem, and Jim Herrington

Leading Congregational Change: A Practical Guide for the Transformational Journey, by Jim Herrington, Mike Bonem, and James H. Furr

The Leader's Journey: Accepting the Call to Personal and Congregational Transformation, by Jim Herrington, Robert Creech, and Trisha Taylor

Culture Shift: Transforming Your Church from the Inside Out, by Robert Lewis and Wayne Cordeiro, with Warren Bird

A New Kind of Christian: A Tale of Two Friends on a Spiritual Journey, by Brian D. McLaren

The Story We Find Ourselves in: Further Adventures of a New Kind of Christian, by Brian D. McLaren

Practicing Greatness: 7 Disciplines of Extraordinary Spiritual Leaders, by Reggie McNeal

The Present Future: Six Tough Questions for the Church, by Reggie McNeal

A Work of Heart: Understanding How God Shapes Spiritual Leaders, by Reggie McNeal

The Millennium Matrix: Reclaiming the Past, Reframing the Future of the Church, by M. Rex Miller

Shaped by God's Heart: The Passion and Practices of Missional Churches, by Milfred Minatrea

The Ascent of a Leader: How Ordinary Relationships Develop Extraordinary Character and Influence, by Bill Thrall, Bruce McNicol, and Ken McElrath

The Elephant in the Boardroom: Speaking the Unspoken About Pastoral Transitions, by Carolyn Weese and J. Russell Crabtree

CONTENTS

ABOUT LEADERSHIP NETWORK

Since 1984, Leadership Network has fostered church innovation and growth by diligently pursuing its far-reaching mission statement: to identify, connect, and help high-capacity Christian leaders multiply their impact.

Although Leadership Network's techniques adapt and change as the Church faces new opportunities and challenges, the organization's work follows a consistent and proven pattern.

Leadership Network brings together entrepreneurial leaders who are focused on similar ministry initiatives. The ensuing collaboration—often across denominational lines—creates a strong base from which individual leaders can better analyze and refine their own strategies. Peer-to-peer interaction, dialogue, and sharing inevitably accelerate participants' innovation and ideas. Leadership Network further enhances this process through developing and distributing highly targeted ministry tools and resources, including audio and video programs, special reports, e-publications, and online downloads.

With Leadership Network's assistance, today's Christian leaders are energized, equipped, inspired, and better able to multiply their own dynamic Kingdom-building initiatives.

Launched in 1996 in conjunction with Jossey-Bass (a Wiley imprint), Leadership Network Publications present thoroughly researched and innovative concepts from leading thinkers, practitioners, and pioneering churches. The series collectively draws from a range of disciplines, with individual titles offering perspective on one or more of five primary areas:

1. Enabling effective leadership

2. Encouraging life-changing service

3. Building authentic community

4. Creating Kingdom-centered impact

5. Engaging cultural and demographic realities

For additional information on the mission or activities of Leadership Network, please contact:

Leadership Network
www.leadnet.org
(800) 765-5323
client.care@leadnet.org

FOREWORD

HIS NAME WAS FRED.

For more than three years, we met almost every Thursday for lunch and then would take a walk. As we walked, I would debrief the week and describe the problems I was working on. We always had plenty to talk about, and many times our conversations got rather animated.

Actually, I was the animated one. Fred listened patiently as I explored the edges of my thoughts and feelings. He offered counsel and insights into our organization and its leader. He helped me understand how to apply my unique set of skills to the situations I faced. He was my coach, friend, and lifeline.

I have told Fred repeatedly that a main reason I have been able to serve as executive pastor of Willow Creek for almost ten years now is because he coached me during my very first years in the job. I absolutely know I would not have made it without his help.

Fred was effective because he had spent years as a first chair leader in the marketplace *and* he had served effectively for five years as a second chair leader in our church. He understood Willow Creek and its culture. He also understood and had worked for our senior pastor, Bill Hybels. (It didn't hurt that Fred was, and still is, an incredibly fun person to be with.)

Over the years I have regularly gotten calls and e-mails from executive pastors asking for my advice on how to be more effective in the role. They have asked me what books or seminars have helped me over the years. I come up empty every time. I don't know of anything that addresses the complexities and tensions that are unique to the second chair role. What I want to tell them is, "Get a Fred!" But folks like Fred are hard to come by.

This is why it is so exciting for me to introduce you to Mike Bonem, Roger Patterson, and *Leading from the Second Chair*.

Drawing on their years of second chair experience, as well as the experience of other skilled second chair leaders, Mike and Roger have captured the essence of the second chair role. *It is about leading and managing your way through a set of paradoxes.* The first time Mike shared the three key paradoxes with me, I immediately knew they were on to something; it rang so true to my experience.

I remember the day I figured out that Bill Hybels wanted me to boldly lead like a first chair leader, not just "manage" the church staff. Yet I had to do so knowing he could step in at any time and reverse a decision I had just made. This was counterintuitive to everything I had ever read about leadership. This is the paradox of subordinate-leader.

As executive pastor, I am expected to know something about everything going on at Willow Creek, and at the same time to provide hands-on leadership of a multimillion-dollar capital campaign, while offering world-class coaching to the high school pastor and a dozen other ministry leaders. The pressure is immense. This is the paradox of deep-wide.

Finally, there have been days when I dreamed intensely about the future of my church. Dreams so real that I am sure God would want them to come alive right away. Yet ultimately my dreams are just one voice in a larger community, under someone else's leadership. I have had to learn to trust God and wait on Him patiently. This is the paradox of contentment-dreaming.

The insights from Mike and Roger are unique, and I believe they will benefit you or anyone in a second chair role, regardless of the size of your church or organization.

But beyond offering lots of practical advice, I believe the book has something else equally valuable. It offers hope, because, you see, the second chair role can be very lonely and there are many days you wish someone would just tell you that you're not crazy. After reading Mike and Roger's story, along with the stories of other second chair leaders, I don't feel quite so alone. I feel understood, and I have more hope.

I pray that all of you can find a Fred in your life as you navigate your second chair role. But in the meantime, it gives me great joy to invite you to journey with Mike and Roger in *Leading from the Second Chair.*

Greg L. Hawkins
Executive Pastor
Willow Creek Community Church

PREFACE

WHEN WE BEGAN a monthly business outreach lunch series two years ago, we (coauthors Mike and Roger) knew we wanted to combine lessons in leadership with biblical principles. To be honest, the first several months were hit-or-miss. As we evaluated one of our misses, we realized we were teaching first chair leadership concepts to a group of middle managers. Shifting our approach to address their needs, we titled the series "Leading from the Second Chair." Their immediate receptiveness told us we had struck a chord.

As we continued to develop the material, we could see that this topic interested many people in the church and the marketplace. Their interest was not due to a lack of material on the broad subject of leadership. Many outstanding resources address the general question, "How can I be a more effective leader?" What they wanted was to have something that addressed their unique challenges. They knew from experience that second chair leadership was different. They wanted to know how to navigate the obstacles they faced in this subordinate role and how to capitalize on the opportunities that seemed just beyond their grasp.

In truth, some of the positive feedback to our original presentations was simply due to our acknowledgment of these issues. We found an audience that wanted validation of their concerns and challenges and that wanted to look forward optimistically to the future. It is in this spirit that we offer this work. It is intended to be a practical and encouraging book for those who faithfully serve in a variety of second chair roles in churches, judicatories, and businesses. You do not need another "how to be a leader" book. You want to improve your leadership with resources that recognize how your role is different from that of senior pastor, executive director, bishop, or CEO. We hope you will find the affirmation and instruction that you need as you read the stories and principles in these pages.

Written from the Second Chair

A book about leading from the second chair should be written by second chair leaders. We both serve in second chair roles at West University Baptist Church, Roger as the associate pastor and Mike as the minister of

discipleship. Roger has also served as the student minister of this congregation and another. Mike's prior experience offers a different perspective
on the second chair. He has been a second chair leader in business, a consultant to businesses and congregations, and a lay leader in the congregations where he was a member. In our formal and informal education
and all of our volunteer and vocational experiences, we have sought to
improve as leaders. More important, we have endeavored to serve God's
Kingdom by offering our best to the churches in which He has placed us.

West University Baptist is a seventy-seven-year-old congregation in an
affluent neighborhood near the center of Houston. Like most churches
with a long history, West University has experienced many seasons of
blessing and growth, but it has also had to deal with periods of decline
and crisis. From 1980 to 1999, West University was in a period of steady
decline, with average weekend attendance falling by 40 percent. Many
factors contributed to this slow erosion of a once-vibrant congregation.

In 1996, the congregation called Barry Landrum as its senior pastor.
Roger came on board in 1997 as the student minister. Mike and his family joined the church in 1998, and he joined the staff in 2001 after leaving his business consulting career. During the five years from 1999 to
2004, God richly blessed West University Baptist and the downward trend
reversed. Average attendance has now increased by 94 percent, and many
other signs of congregational health are evident. We do not say this to
take credit for the "success" of the church; we give God alone glory for
the quantitative results and, more important, the changed lives. Nor are
we saying that we were the only second chair leaders at West University
during these years. The church has been faithfully served by our colleagues
on the staff and by a host of lay leaders, too many to name. In fact, this
broad group of second chair leaders underscores one of the themes of this
book. When a group of leaders is willing to be used by God and is unified in following His vision, exciting things happen.

The ideas and recommendations in this book grow out of our own experiences as second chair leaders, as fellow travelers and learners in the journey of leadership. The simplistic snapshot of West University Baptist
presented here may leave the impression that we have enjoyed unqualified
success and an easy journey. There have been many joyous moments and
ample victories, and we feel blessed to work in such a positive environment.

But there have also been many struggles. We had "great ideas" that
failed—some that never got off the ground because they were not supported
by the first chair, and others that did get off the ground and should not
have. There were times when we bridled at the restraints imposed by our

positions. At other times, we stepped too close to the line where constructive dissent becomes insubordination. We had to negotiate (and renegotiate) working arrangements, apologize for missteps, and accept solutions that we thought were less-than-ideal. Leading from the second chair has not been easy for us, but it has still been one of the most rewarding seasons of our lives.

Beyond Our Experiences

The lessons and principles embodied in this book are not limited to our experiences. We are indebted to a number of second chair leaders who shared their stories—both positive and negative—as we developed this project. Our conversation with more than a dozen individuals, all of whom have significant second chair experience, added depth and richness to our work. Steve Ahlquist, Tom Billings, Kelli Caskey, Gary Ferbet, Dena Harrison, Greg Hawkins, Ric Hodgin, Bob Johnson, Dian Kidd, Kim Miller, Preston Mitchell, Robert Moore, Dan Reiland, Warren Schuh, Glenn Smith, Robin Smith, and Geoff Surratt have all learned valuable lessons in the second chair and were glad to pass them along to others. More information on these second chair leaders is in the back of this book.

As you will see in our definition, a second chair leader does not have to fit a particular mold or hold a particular title, and this was certainly true for the individuals with whom we spoke. Beyond the common denominator of the second chair, they had little in common in their backgrounds and roles. They served in small and large churches, judicatories, and other organizations, and they covered the spectrum of denominations. They were men and women. Some saw the second chair as their lifelong calling, while others saw it as a step on their way to a first chair role. Some were not sure where God might lead them. Many had titles that clearly indicated their second chair role, but not all did.

Our outside interviews did more than furnish interesting stories. They confirmed the challenges of second chair leadership, and they validated our framework. Being in the second chair is the ultimate leadership paradox. It is the paradox of being a leader and a subordinate, having a deep role and a wide one, and being content with the present while continuing to dream about the future. Some may say it is impossible to do all these things, but we found that effective second chair leaders embrace these extremes. Those who thrive in this role, whether for a season or for the long run, learn to live with the tension that this creates. It is the tensions and paradoxes of second chair leadership that we explore in this book.

A Word to First Chairs

This book is written with second chair leaders in mind, but it will also be a useful tool for those in the first chair. If you are the senior pastor or executive director or are in some other top role, we hope you will gain new insights into your second chairs' attitudes and actions. Most of you sat in a second chair role at one time, but you may have forgotten what it was like. Perhaps the ideas presented on these pages will start a dialogue between the two of you, a dialogue that will benefit you, the second chair, and your ministry as a whole.

Each paradox concludes with a special section called "A Word to First Chairs." Here we apply the principles of the paradox to the role of the first chair. Some first chairs are missing the benefit and support of a capable second chair because they are hesitant to allow the latter to lead. For each paradox, you can take steps that will be of great benefit for your subordinates. But before you take these steps, you need to decide if you are willing for your direct reports to be true leaders, if you are ready to release them to the challenge at hand. Your second chairs are living with the tensions of the paradoxes. We want to encourage you to help them thrive, rather than just survive, in their role.

Tension and paradox are not necessarily bad. They are a reality we live with. They force us to stretch and reexamine our assumptions. Once we recognize them, they can propel us to a place of greater success. If you are in the second chair, you have not been called to a place of comfort; you have been called to a place of leadership. As you learn and grow in this experience, you have the opportunity to become more effective as a leader and to be used by God in a powerful way. We hope that you will be encouraged today to be the leader that God has called you to be, and that much Kingdom fruit will result from your faithful commitment.

LIVING IN THE PARADOXES

THE SECOND CHAIR is a complex and challenging role to fill, but you probably already know that. You understand the tension of leadership and the high-stakes game that goes along with it. Since you have picked up this book, you know that serving in the second chair involves seasons of frustration and stress as you try to follow your senior leader. Because of your position and your natural temperament, you cannot be passive about the future of your church or organization. At the same time, your position seems to limit your ability to change things for the better. This book is written for you, if you are looking for hope and direction as you live with this sense of urgency and passion.

This is not just another leadership book. At times, we have felt great exhilaration in discovering resources that helped shape our vision of a preferred future or offered a solution to a burdensome problem. We have been frequent consumers of books, tapes, and conferences as a means of improving our leadership. Yet we have often felt frustration or discouragement after using these resources because they were not aimed at us. Their focus was the senior leader of the organization, the person who has the freedom and relative autonomy that comes with this top position. In the second chair, the amount of change you can initiate is limited because you are not the vision caster, the lead leader.

You may have speculated, in moments of frustration or dreaming, that things would be different if you could have the reins, just for a season. You are sure that your communication style would be more effective, your handling of staff issues would shine, and bold new initiatives would be launched. You know that you would make the tough calls that need to be made, and at the same time you would win the world with your charisma. At some level, you may be chomping at the bit to move into the role of the first chair. It is only natural that you feel this way; it is not a bad reflection on you or the leader that you follow. As one who is called to lead, it is simply the reality of how God has wired you.

Or you may never have imagined yourself in the first chair. You have neither the desire to make the tough calls nor the charisma to charm the masses. But you envision your organization becoming much more effective, much different than it is currently, and accomplishing far more as a result. You know that you hold a key position, and you want to be part of a great, enduring enterprise that is fulfilling its God-given calling and potential.

Whichever scenario you identify with, the good news is this resource has been written just for you! We want you to understand that you are not alone. God desires to use this experience in the second chair as a transforming season in your life. As you read this book, we hope you become aware that God has a specific role for you to play, and incredible potential for you to realize. This role challenges your ego, buffers your speech, and keeps you anchored in your calling. It is a place of growth and development, a place of real contribution, and a place that tests your commitment. God wants your best wherever you are, no matter the circumstances, no matter the comfort level of your chair. To put it bluntly, the chair in which you sit is not a La-Z-Boy! It is often the most uncomfortable chair in the room, but it can be deeply fulfilling.

What Is a Second Chair Leader? — *market language*

A second chair leader is *a person in a subordinate role whose influence with others adds value throughout the organization.* This is a definition that we will break down and reinforce as we seek ways to put it into practice. Think about it: even though you are not in the first chair, your actions can change the entire organization for the better. Of course, you may struggle with the idea of subordination, or think it impossible to have an impact throughout the organization. Each term in this definition has multiple shades of meaning, but the second chair leaders with whom we spoke consistently demonstrated this picture.

Second chair leadership is unique because it is not strictly based on the power and authority of positional leadership. A person who is able to succeed by influencing others is a more effective leader than one who issues edicts to be obeyed. Leading from the second chair requires this kind of pure leadership because it seeks to improve the entire organization, from the first chair to the last, without the formal authority of being the first chair leader. Of course, most second chair leaders do have some degree of positional authority. Those who thrive, however, find much of their success through influence and relationships. They bring a new perspective to the powerful concept of servant leadership.

You do not have to be the number two person in an organizational hierarchy to be a second chair leader. In fact, our definition can include anyone who is not the lead leader. Every organization has a perceived pecking order. In reality, your position may be tenth chair, or seventh, or third. In nearly any position on the totem pole, you are a *potential* second chair leader—a person in a subordinate role *who has an opportunity* to influence others and add value throughout the organization. You alone can choose how to develop and cultivate your influence for the benefit of the congregation. Regardless of where you are on the leadership development journey, there is room to grow and learn.

The distinction between hierarchical position on an organization chart and true second chair leadership is illustrated in the executive branch of the federal government. It is obvious that the president is the first chair leader, and the vice president has the official second chair position. In many administrations, however, the vice president's actual role is relatively insignificant. Which positions in the cabinet and the office of the president are the key second chair roles? Who has the most influence in setting and directing the national political agenda?

It depends. It changes from one administration to the next. Some of this is driven by pressing national issues—the economy, domestic security, international affairs—but the bigger determinant is the individual's relationship with the first chair (the president) and the individual's ability to work with others to influence the broader political landscape. This is the true picture of second chair leadership. A trusted chief of staff or press secretary can be a powerful figure, even if his or her official responsibilities and departmental budget seem to be much less than those of the secretaries of the treasury or defense.

Of course, even the first chair leader answers to someone: a board, the elders, shareholders, a bishop, the voters. Ultimately, in Christ's Kingdom, we are all in the second chair, submitting to Christ as the head. But for those who do not occupy the top position, the ways to lead effectively are distinctly different. These differences can be summarized in three apparent paradoxes that second chair leaders encounter throughout their careers.

Three Paradoxes in the Second Chair

A second chair leader's unique role involves a special set of tensions. Any leadership position has challenges that stretch the individual, but these general stresses are not our focus. The unique tensions for a second chair arise because the expectations he encounters appear to be incompatible, or even contradictory. He is expected to be a bold initiator and faithful follower, a creative thinker and detailed implementer. The ongoing challenge is to do a variety of tasks and do them well. Being called upon to wear so many hats can be perplexing and stressful. We describe these tensions as the three apparent paradoxes of second chair leadership: *subordinate-leader, deep-wide*, and *contentment-dreaming*. They are paradoxes because at first glance they seem to be mutually exclusive. But our contention is that these pairs do not represent either-or choices. Rather, effective second chair leaders need to live within each paradox and master both ends of the spectrum. Some may experience the tension of one paradox more intensely than another, but all three paradoxes are woven into the fabric of being a second chair leader.

In *Built to Last*, Jim Collins and Jerry Porras contrast the "Tyranny of the *or*" with the "Genius of the *and*." They explain that businesses trapped by either-or thinking are not nearly as successful as those that insist on finding a way to achieve *both-and* (Collins and Porras, 1994). Some companies decide they must choose between producing a high-quality product or one that is low-cost, but those that find a way to do both have long-term success. Some church leaders believe they must focus on evangelism or on discipleship, on reaching new members or on caring for the current flock. The ones that have enduring impact for the Kingdom discover a way to accomplish both-and. In the same way, effective second chair leaders discover the genius of the *and* in each of the three paradoxes.

The first is the subordinate-leader paradox. For many of us, our mental model of leadership involves having complete freedom to set direction and determine actions for ourselves and the organization without any "interference" from a supervisor. From this perspective, any submission to another person is less leaderlike. Effective second chair leaders do not have this sort of zero-sum view of organizational responsibility. They know that two heads are better than one, and that the first chair is not an adversary. They are able to lead without being at the top of the pyramid. Most important, they understand that their authority and effectiveness as a second chair stem from a healthy, subordinate relationship with their first chair.

The second challenge is abbreviated as the deep-wide paradox. Second chair leaders have specific roles that are narrower and deeper in scope than those of the first chair, yet they need to have a broad, organization-wide perspective. Some who struggle with this paradox resent the restrictions of their role as being too narrow, or they see the more detailed dirty work as being beneath them. At the other extreme, some excel at their specific tasks but fail to see the big picture. If an issue arises, they always see it from the viewpoint of how it affects their ministry. Narrow leaders may have trouble negotiating the informal relational networks that are leveraged by second chairs who seek to have a broader impact on the organization. Effective second chair leaders develop the skills to be both deep and wide.

The final paradox is described by the tension of contentment-dreaming. Being the second chair does not mean giving up on individual or corporate dreams. But a dream cannot be allowed to become shortsighted ambition, nor can it be positioned in competition with the plans of the first chair. Second chair leaders intentionally seek to shape the organization's direction and mesh their individual dreams with the broader vision. They understand that an apparent detour from their dream may be short-term and even a catalyst to fulfilling their God-given potential. Successful second chair leaders are able to maintain contentment with the present without losing their sense of God-given calling for their future.

The three paradoxes represent daily tensions for a second chair leader. These are not tensions she chooses but the reality of her position and temperament. Although each paradox is present to some degree for every second chair, a leader's specific situation or personality may lead to extra stress in one of the three. In the pages that follow, you will meet an executive pastor whose hard lessons in his initial second chair role enabled him to embrace the subordinate-leader paradox when he returned to a similar role years later. Another executive pastor found the deep-wide paradox to be the essence of second chair leadership as he frequently stepped into interim and special-project roles, all the while keeping the big picture in mind. You will meet the copastor of a church plant who nurtured God's vision for several years while faithfully serving in an earlier, challenging ministry setting. She learned that contentment and dreaming can coexist. You will be introduced to a visionary leader who wrestled with all three of the paradoxes as he used his exceptional musical gifts.

The second chair requires a special leadership lens that brings clarity to the challenges of the three paradoxes. The lens must be trifocal, allowing you to focus on how you manage your relationships (subordinate-leader paradox), your work habits (deep-wide paradox), and your emotions (contentment-dreaming paradox). As you see and understand more clearly the tensions experienced in the paradoxes, you will be better equipped to navigate your way through them. Being better equipped, you will become a better leader, making a more significant contribution to God's Kingdom.

Being a second chair leader is full of challenges, but they are not insurmountable. As you will see in the stories of successful second chairs, it is possible to discover the genius of the *and*. They are loyal subordinates and high-impact leaders. They accomplish their specific responsibilities with excellence while maintaining a broad perspective and seeking the best for the entire organization. They find contentment and personal growth in their present role while continuing to listen for how God plans to use them and see them prosper in the future. It is these paradoxes that we explore throughout the remainder of this book.

The Importance of Second Chair Leaders

Is a book specifically for second chair leaders really needed? One simple answer is, "Do the math!" It is obvious that the population of second chair leaders is much larger than that of first chair leaders. This fact alone makes a strong case for designing resources for second chair leaders.

The real reasons, however, are much deeper. For any organization to function at its highest level of performance, it must have effective leaders in second chair roles. A compelling explanation of this point comes, again, from management expert Jim Collins. His research in *Good to Great* shows that the organization operating as "a genius with a thousand helpers" will not have sustained success (Collins, 2001). Organizations that follow this philosophy have many people in second chair positions who are not allowed to be *leaders*. In contrast with this model, Collins's research shows that organizations should focus first on building a strong and broad base of leadership. In other words, second chair leaders need to be in place and allowed to lead if a church is going to have enduring success.

In our interviews, we found many second chair leaders who made a significant contribution to their organization, in a variety of ways. Kim Miller took the idea of using the arts in worship and developed a creative, integrated worship experience that has become a central part of Ginghamsburg Church's identity. Warren Schuh led a major restructuring of Calvary Community Church that was "like turning a DC-3 into a 747." Dian Kidd's pragmatic nature played an important role in bringing Union Baptist Association's blue-sky thinking back down to earth. Glenn Smith was the driving force as Sugar Creek Baptist initiated and developed a church planting movement. Can second chair leaders make a difference in their organization? These stories, and others you will read, show that they can have an organization-shaping influence. As Preston Mitchell, of Fellowship Church in Dallas, said, "There are people gifted to be second chair leaders. We are the people who make it happen, and it is a joy to do it."

We recognize that you might consider your current position to be an intermediate point in the leadership journey. You might use a less positive description for "intermediate point"; perhaps you consider it an unnecessary, unproductive delay. Your gifts and your sense of calling point toward a "better" chair—either a first chair role or a second chair position with considerably more responsibility. One purpose of this book is to encourage you to be patient and learn as much as you can in your current role. Too many leaders focus all their energy on moving to the next chair as quickly as possible, and they miss the opportunity to develop their gifts in the current chair.

After Mike completed his master's degree in business, he was convinced that a first chair business role was the only goal worth pursuing. At one critical decision point in his career journey, he sought guidance from a trusted advisor. Over the course of several conversations, this man helped Mike see that his personal dreams and strengths might be best suited for a number two role rather than the corner office. This became a liberating idea that allowed God to continue redefining Mike's ambitions and his identity. Whatever your current or future chair may be, you can learn valuable lessons today that will have long-lasting benefits. An attitude of contentment and a desire to learn are foundational elements of effective second chair leadership.

Second chair leadership, as we have defined it, is also biblical. Few books on leadership emphasize the concepts of subordination, adding value for the benefit of others, and developing influence without formal authority. But this is exactly the style of leadership that is modeled by Jesus and repeatedly taught in the New Testament. It is the style of leadership needed in the church. Bill Hybels, senior pastor of Willow Creek Community Church, says, "There is nothing like the local church when it's working right" (Hybels, 2002, p. 23). We would add, "And when it's working right, the attitudes and practices of second chair leadership are firmly in place." Simply stated, today's churches and businesses would have far fewer problems if the leaders—first and second chair—adopted these traits.

Second Chair Leaders in the Church

This book is written first and foremost with the church in mind, but the concepts of effective second chair leadership are applicable in any organization. This includes nonprofits and for-profits, volunteer-based organizations and businesses with paid employees, multilayered enterprises and smaller ones. If your organization involves at least a handful of people, it is likely to have one or more second chair leaders.

When we look at a congregation, we encounter the same problems as in a business plus a few added wrinkles. A congregation is a complex entity because it includes both paid and volunteer leaders who have diverse opinions about the organization's ultimate purposes and the best means for achieving them. A business has a bottom-line to measure against, but what is a congregation's bottom line? In the same way, the *who* and *how* questions of congregational leadership can be very confusing. Some congregations cannot answer the question, "Who is the first chair leader?" In other churches, the pervasive culture insists that only ordained clergy can be leaders. Still others find it difficult to make a major decision because of a confusing structure or cumbersome approval process. Effectively leading the average congregation in America is every bit as challenging as corporate leadership. Unfortunately, the church has been slow to accept the need for a higher level of leadership from an expanded base of leaders.

It is no wonder, then, that the majority of congregations in America are struggling. The flat or declining attendance trend of many congregations and burnout among clergy are clear indicators of a problem. Lack of a broad, effective core of leaders is a critical factor in this stagnation. Yet the implicit approach that many churches employ is a variation of the "one genius" model. The senior pastor imparts all the ideas and is responsible for giving direction, and the members and other staff are expected to accept and implement. For the church to further grow in its redemptive potential, a new wave of second chair leaders is essential, men and women who work in concert with their first chair leaders to accomplish the mission that God has placed before them. The potential second chairs who are waiting in the wings need to step forward, and the first chairs need to encourage and empower them.

Effective second chair leaders in the church understand God's vision for their congregation, and they embrace it wholeheartedly. They are able to see ways to accelerate progress toward the vision. They can design and implement new ministries and overhaul old ones to keep the congregation on track. They can share the vision with others and expand the foundation of committed leaders and followers. They can lift the leadership burden from the first chair without usurping authority.

The same needs and opportunities exist outside the church as well. Denominational entities, parachurch ministries, and businesses need to increase the depth of their leadership bench. The lead leader needs other capable leaders if the organization is to accomplish its vision. Any entity that seeks to increase its impact and its effectiveness needs second chair leaders.

The World's Greatest Second Chair Leader

"You shall be in charge of my palace, and all my people are to submit to your orders. Only with respect to the throne will I be greater than you" (Genesis 41:40).

There it is, the climax of the story! It is one of the greatest comebacks ever! Do you remember the young man who was known by his brothers as a dreamer, the one who wore the beautifully ornamented coat given to him by his father to signify his status as most favored? This young, arrogant dreamer was thrown into the bottom of a well and sold into slavery by these same brothers. Then, as a foreigner and former prisoner, he attained a rank of leadership that no other Hebrew in all of history has enjoyed. We do not know all that happened to Joseph, only what the Scripture reveals. But this is enough to show that his journey included some of the lowest lows and highest highs that life can offer.

For Joseph to finish as he did, a light bulb must have turned on somewhere along the way. There must have been a season when he discovered the meaning of second chair leadership. As a child in Canaan, Joseph showed no understanding of subordination; he expected his older brothers to bow to him. Nor did he grasp the subtleties of influencing others; all he needed to do was run to his daddy to get what he wanted. It was certainly not on his agenda to add value to the organization of Jacob and Sons, Inc.; he only cared about himself.

Life as a slave and as a prisoner taught Joseph many lessons. He was in a foreign land with a foreign language. He was no longer the favored son in his household. He had no position of authority. To survive this harsh environment, he had to find a way to set himself apart. So with no other choice, Joseph grew up. He apparently learned quickly and retained these lessons for the rest of his life.

What did Joseph learn and apply that set him apart? What principles can we glean from this great leader to foster our growth and development as second chair leaders? What can we learn from him that will strengthen and encourage us in our journey of service to our God? As we share from our personal experiences and those of others, we also seek to learn about the challenges and opportunities of second chair leadership from one of the best second chair leaders of all time, Joseph.

Wherever you serve, we hope that you will be inspired to honor God in all your ways. We pray that God will enrich your day-to-day living as

you find greater purpose and motivation to lead and serve in His Kingdom. Joseph discovered a much greater purpose in Egypt, and we have
found joy in discovering God's purposes in our own second chair roles.

Reinhold Niebuhr's "Serenity Prayer" is an apt prescription for any second chair leader: "God grant me the serenity to accept the things I cannot change, courage to change the things I can, and the wisdom to know
the difference." As you read the chapters that follow, we hope you will
learn from some of our mistakes, and find reassurance and encouragement
in others. Now that you know the end of the story, let's see what it takes
to realize the full potential of effective leadership in the second chair.

2

AM I A SECOND CHAIR LEADER?

YOU KNOW YOUR TITLE and your official responsibilities. On that basis, it may seem easy to determine if you fill a second chair role. At the same time, you may wonder, "Am I a second chair leader?" It is the *leader* part of the equation that causes you to pause and reflect. As you consider our definition, you may wonder if you truly have influence with others that adds value throughout the organization.

As we said in the previous chapter, leading from the second chair is pure leadership because it seeks to improve the entire organization without the positional power of being in the first chair. Dan Reiland refers to this as the "all authority, no authority" paradox. The expectations placed on many second chairs seem to be commensurate with the full authority of a first chair, but the reality is that they often have limited formal authority. The key to leading in a subordinate role is identifying and understanding opportunities to cultivate influence each and every day. You may have great potential but are just beginning to develop this broader influence. Or you may have begun the second chair journey but are not achieving the level of influence and success you would like. In either case, the question that remains is, "What do I do now?"

Influence: The Leader's Building Block

If you believe lack of authority prevents you from leading effectively, it is time to rethink your understanding of leadership. John Maxwell says, "Leadership is influence, nothing more, nothing less" (1998b, p. 13). Maxwell and others depict how this influence is expanded or diminished, describing it as a kind of "leadership bank account." When leaders come into an organization, they are given a certain amount of "leadership capital" in their account. Most people in the organization give the newcomer the benefit of the doubt; the capital in the account gives the new person the permission and freedom required to lead. It is seen in the willingness of people to follow when the leader starts a new ministry or begins to make changes. But even in this honeymoon stage, the organization is looking to see how the leader will invest this capital. Each decision adds to or subtracts from the bank account. As you make wise decisions, give sound counsel, and understand the implications of your choices, you make deposits into your account and the balance rises. If you are seen as a team player and a team builder, willing to set aside your own agenda for the sake of the entire organization, your account increases even more. This becomes a virtuous cycle. Each deposit increases your influence, which allows you to make more significant decisions in the future.

On the other hand, if you make poor leadership decisions or take too much risk without allowing for significant input and feedback, you spend the capital in your leadership account and diminish your influence. If you continually express insubordination toward your first chair, your influence is diminished because you are seen as untrustworthy in major decisions or difficult times. This can become a vicious, downward cycle. A leader may sense a loss of capital and try harder to maintain influence by forcing decisions prematurely or inappropriately. This lowers the account and influence even further.

The lesson to learn: long-term, successful leadership is based on influence that is developed through strong relationships and wise decisions in ministry. Kim Miller, creative director of Ginghamsburg Church, has lived the lesson of leadership influence. When Kim first came to Ginghamsburg, she got involved in children's musicals because she had held similar volunteer roles in other churches. A year later, the church was preparing to move into a new facility that was equipped for a full range of multimedia presentations. Kim was invited to a meeting to plan the opening weekend at the new site, and she left with the assignment of creating and producing a skit called "The Broody Bunch Goes to Church."

Because of the success of this skit and Senior Pastor Mike Slaughter's desire to create an integrated worship experience, Kim's influence began to increase. In her words, "They kept inviting me back" to worship planning meetings. Before long, she was volunteering every Wednesday in the role. It took time before the significance of her role and her influence became apparent. In her early days, one staff member told her, "This will never, ever be a real job for you." Kim is now one of six people on the church's senior management team. One important aspect of leadership influence is highlighted by her philosophy: those "who keep using their gifts every day work themselves into a job." Said another way, using your gifts and building strong relationships are high-yield ways to increase the leadership bank account.

One reality is that influence is harder to obtain for second chairs than it is for first chairs. Preaching weekly sermons, guiding congregationwide decisions, and participating in key leadership groups gives the senior pastor high visibility. An executive director of an organization has frequent contact with staff, board members, and outside constituents. As a result, influence for first chairs accrues more quickly and at a much greater level than for someone who fills a secondary role. Second chairs may have deeper influence in certain areas, but it takes longer for them to build broad organizational influence.

Just because it takes longer, however, does not mean that influence building is less important for a second chair leader. How much credibility do you have with the people who are affected by your ministry? Do they see you as someone they trust at a deep level? This includes your senior leader, volunteer workers, fellow staff members, people in your congregation, and those you are trying to reach. Without credibility and trust in their eyes, you will not have influence. Building credibility requires patience, consistency, and persistence. It requires a spirit of teamwork and cooperation. You are not competing with your senior leader or the others on your team; seeing them as competitors is a dead-end road. Building credibility and influence requires putting the prestige of your position aside and picking up the towel of service. You must commit to serving your entire organization well, each and every day. Then, and only then, will your peers, subordinates, and senior leader truly allow you to lead from the second chair.

Influence is the most important leadership building block in a second chair's toolkit. Those who learn this lesson and practice it daily begin to make great strides in their leadership journey. Those who ignore this lesson will someday wonder why their voice is not being heard. If this happens to you, you can be sure you will miss out on many opportunities to maximize your God-given potential. The choice is yours. Begin now by choosing to cultivate influence throughout the organization.

Unpacking the Definition

We have focused on influence, but leading from the second chair is more than that. What does it mean to be "a person in a subordinate role whose influence with others adds value throughout the organization"? We can learn more about second chair leadership by unpacking this definition one piece at a time.

A *Subordinate*  *I react to this. Why?*

Even the most gifted or capable second chair is still under the leadership and authority of another leader. Even though some organizations are more egalitarian than hierarchical, every second chair we interviewed recognized this difference between the two roles. Being in a subordinate position often causes tension for a second chair. At times, you will disagree with your first chair's decision or be frustrated by the lack of one. Or you may wonder why you are not given more responsibility. It helps when your first chair provides an explanation, but sometimes you have to be satisfied with telling yourself, "She is the first chair and I'm the subordinate. This is her decision to make."

When Robert Moore was called to Christ the King Lutheran, his goal was "to be a good subordinate, tell the truth [to his senior pastor] behind closed doors, and work well at my job." He understood that the congregation looks for only one person to be the ultimate leader and that "I was going to be successful if I made the senior pastor successful." He made sure his language and actions acknowledged the leadership of his first chair. This did not negate Robert's own significant leadership role; in fact, he ultimately succeeded the senior pastor. But Robert's attitude in the second chair is a clear example of our definition of being subordinate. How well are you doing under someone else's authority?

Whose Influence

As we have already described, influence is a second chair's most valuable tool. It is the quality that sets you apart as a leader even as you serve in a subordinate role. You may not have control over your place on the organization chart or your title, but you can expand your influence. Influence is evident in people's readiness to follow you and their desire to include you in key decisions and initiatives.

In Baptist life, each church is autonomous and voluntarily participates in the various denominational entities. A denominational leader has little formal authority, and a second chair in a regional body has even less. Despite this, Dian Kidd of Union Baptist Association has been extremely effective in her role because she understands the principle of influence. Her influence grows out of her passion for the association's vision, her competence in critical areas, and her relationships with many key church leaders. Are you becoming a person with significant influence?

With Others

Leadership is relational. Any leadership role involves a broad network of relationships, with many people, all of the time. Influence without other people is a meaningless concept. In God's Kingdom, relationships are critically important. It is obvious, then, that successful second chair leaders must excel at relationships. These relationships are driven by much more than charisma or a good first impression. They are based on integrity and delivering on promises. They are based on genuine care for others. For some second chairs, building relationships is easy and natural; for others it is hard work, but for all it is essential.

Kelli Caskey of Crossroads Community Church invests heavily in relationships with others. A significant part of her time is spent developing relationships and discipling individuals or couples. She particularly focuses on "identifying Timothys," those individuals in her congregation who have great leadership potential. How would you rate your relationships with the others in your area of responsibility?

Adds Value

Is the church or ministry you serve better because of your influence? Adding value has many facets. It may be seen in better information for decision making or in more creativity in programs. A second chair may add value by strengthening team relations or being a sounding board for a colleague. Desiring to add value means always looking for ways to improve the organization, seeking to help by showing genuine interest in the ministries of other peers and assisting wherever a contribution can be made. This is service arising from a servant's heart, not self-serving motives.

At the beginning of 2004, Bob Johnson made the unusual move of leaving a successful senior pastorate to become the executive pastor of Chapelwood United Methodist. After prayerful consideration, he saw this as an opportunity to add great value. In his first year, he helped clarify the church's vision, accelerated its shift to a "lay led culture," and added structure that the organization needed. As an ordained minister and former senior pastor, he is a sounding board and an involved guide for the rest of the pastoral staff. Do you stop what you are doing to add value and help others?

Throughout the Organization

Second chairs who are committed to cultivating influence and adding value have the opportunity to make the entire organization better. Some seize it, but others stay focused on a narrow ministry area. The habit of looking across the broader organization is a distinguishing trait of second chair leaders. They may not be involved in every decision or every ministry, but their perspective is organizationwide. They are able to add value throughout.

Steve Ahlquist leads the part of North Coast Church that is rarely seen by members. Despite this, he helps instill a sense of excitement and commitment in this group by showing how their excellence in technology, facilities management, and financial matters contributes to everything that is being done at North Coast. In what ways do you affect throughout?

The Faces of the Second Chair

Second chair leaders can be found in any organization. Some have titles that clearly indicate their role, but many do not. Two titles that are often associated with second chair leadership in a multistaff church are executive pastor and associate pastor. Some individuals serving in such a role are seminary-trained clergy, while others are businesspeople who have made a midcareer transition. Some see themselves as future first chair leaders-in-training, and others feel called to long-term ministry in the second chair. These roles require insight, expertise, and leadership ability. They often carry a larger burden than other staff positions do because of their breadth of responsibility. Dan Reiland observes that once "many churches had passed 1,000 in attendance, a new need arose. The senior pastor could no longer keep up with all the demand of staff, infrastructure and ministry design; and at the same time cast vision, remain fresh and creative in the pulpit, raise big dollars, etc. There became a need . . . to divide his job in half" (Reiland, 2002, p. 1; the article is quoted by permission from Dan Reiland's free monthly e-newsletter, "The Pastor's Coach," available at www.INJOY.com).

The executive or associate pastor is not the only second chair leader in a church. Other second chair leaders in your congregation may have any number of titles or roles. In a multistaff church, other pastoral and program staff could be second chair leaders. We also know that it does not take a paycheck to be a leader in a congregation. Second chair leaders may be found in the congregation's key decision-making body: deacons, elders, session, church council, vestry. Or they may lead specific ministries and have widespread influence in doing so. Some lay leaders have enormous influence despite their lack of a significant title or formal role. A person's position may be a platform from which to lead, but a title is not what makes someone an effective second chair leader. When you look again at the definition, it is clear that many people in a congregation are potential second chair leaders.

It may be easiest to define second chair leadership by way of some real examples. If your church is anything like ours, you already know of at least a handful of second chair leaders. These are people who are adding value and cultivating influence in ways that benefit the whole church. What are the pathways for becoming a second chair leader? We answer this by looking at several individuals in the life of West University Baptist and the underlying factors that gave them the influence to be second chair leaders.

Title, or position, is one pathway to the second chair. Roger has the title of associate pastor, which is clearly a second chair role in our church. When he was moved into this role after serving three years as student minister, he immediately took on new responsibilities and built new relationships that increased his influence in the organization. Roger was already developing many second chair practices before his new role, but the change in title accelerated his development as a second chair leader.

Ronny Barner was West University's minister of music and administration for more than thirty-six years. You could say he was a second chair leader by *tenure.* Even though he was a talented musician who led a highly successful music ministry, he was an associate pastor first. He carried a heavy load of counseling, performed weddings and funerals, and provided a significant amount of staff oversight and leadership. The deep relationships he formed over the years and the congregation's respect for Ronny enabled him to be a key component in this church's ability to sustain itself through difficult seasons.

Gary Pennington is a "good ol' boy" from Shreveport, Louisiana, who played a vital leadership role as deacon chair when a former senior pastor resigned abruptly. *Timing* was a significant factor in Gary's ability to fill a critical second chair role. Gary and his wife, Jean, had consistently served the church in many capacities and developed relationships throughout the congregation over a number of years. When the crisis hit, God used Gary to help bring calm and stability to a chaotic situation. Gary led the deacons and the church to seek the heart of God. He became the de facto leader during a time devoid of first chair leadership. It was a deeply stressful period for the church and the Penningtons, but God's perfect timing placed the right person in the right role to lead His flock through the turmoil.

Craig Ward's *talent* placed him in the second chair at West University for a season. Craig has spent a majority of his professional life in the construction industry. When the church set out to redesign and renovate its current facility, Craig offered his expertise and services. He was given the formal responsibility of building and grounds committee chair. As we moved from planning to actual construction, we realized that the scope of the project was much too great for Roger (as the staff assignee) to handle. Craig again dedicated his time to serve the church—training Roger, giving oversight to the project, and finding substantial savings along the way. Throughout the project, Craig showed a second chair leader's perspective, always seeking the best solutions for the church as a whole and working closely with people throughout the organization. In the midst of a difficult season in his own professional life, Craig added tremendous value in a desperately needed role. His true impact throughout the church was realized on the day the facility was opened and dedicated.

Charlotte Landrum is the wife of our senior pastor, and she also leads the church's women's ministry. She is a second chair leader in her own right, primarily due to her remarkable personal *touch*. ChaCha, as she is affectionately known by the kids and many adults, builds deep relationships with people throughout the congregation. She is a trusted friend and counselor, someone who can always be counted on to listen, offer support, and roll up her sleeves to get the job done. Her investment in others adds great value, and it gives her a full leadership bank account that she can draw upon at any time. (transactional language

Mike's title, minister of discipleship, is not automatically associated with second chair leadership. Part of what makes Mike a second chair leader is his *temperament* and his *tenacity*. Tenacity is a nice way of saying that he is opinionated and has a hard time keeping his mouth shut. He wants the church to be the very best it can be. When something slips through the cracks or a program is not running well, he speaks up. When a ministry leader needs a fresh idea, he is quick to offer input. Tenacity can be a valuable trait, but it can also lead to hurt feelings if it is not managed with care. Those who are second chair leaders by virtue of temperament and tenacity can be found doing any job because their contribution is not defined by their title.

A leadership temperament is a common characteristic of all the individuals we have just described, not just Mike. Those with a leader's temperament have a strong desire for the ministry to reach its fullest potential, and they always work toward that goal. "Let someone else worry about it" is not in their vocabulary. They dream big dreams about the things that

God is going to do in the larger organization, and they stand ready to do their part when God creates the opportunity.

Title, tenure, timing, talent, touch, tenacity, temperament: many factors can contribute to a person becoming a second chair leader. Some are within your control, some are not. But even if circumstances put you into a potential second chair role, the choice to cultivate influence with others and become a true second chair leader is yours to make. *discuss how people become 2nd chair leaders*

The Choices of the Second Chair

Joseph found himself in a place where he had to make a choice. The initial set of circumstances that pointed toward a great future had vanished. Even though most of the factors indicated Joseph had no future as a leader, he chose to excel. We do not know exactly how he made this choice, but it related to his stewardship of his relationship with God and with his master in Egypt. Genesis 39:2–4 tell us: "The Lord was with Joseph and he prospered, and he lived in the house of his Egyptian master. When his master saw that the Lord was with him and that the Lord gave him success in everything he did, Joseph found favor in his eyes, and became his attendant."

Joseph, the favorite son who was sold into slavery by his brothers, prospered in these difficult circumstances. You would think that a slave would lose all hope and would have no desire to achieve. Joseph enjoyed the favor of God, but he also made the choice to do his best. How else would you explain the phrase, "the Lord gave him success in everything he did"? God does not force anyone to be successful. "Everything" is not a one-time occurrence. It shows a pattern of faithfulness and persistence. Over time, Joseph was faithful to the new authority in his life, and he was given favor from God. Potiphar was a shrewd leader who sought to maximize his resources by putting Joseph into a place of administration and leadership in his home. Joseph's choice to honor his God and do his tasks with diligence and excellence led him to a place of great influence. Even though the deck seemed stacked against him, Joseph chose to use the talent and tenacity that God had given him to serve with excellence and ultimately become a model of second chair leadership.

Whatever factors may have placed you in a position to be a second chair leader, you still have a choice to make. Will you seek to develop relationships and expand your influence? If you want to be a person whose influence with others adds value throughout the organization, consider four specific choices.

Choice One: Put on Leadership Lenses

An early and important choice Roger made as he was promoted into the role of associate pastor continues to shape his approach to ministry and leadership. The choice? No matter what the challenge, he tries to step back and look at every problem or opportunity through leadership lenses. This is the perspective you have as you look at a given situation and try to see an issue as your first chair would see it, keeping the overall needs of the organization in mind. It affects the way you process information, make decisions, and prioritize your time.

like going to the balcony

If you want to have the best vision you can, you ask an ophthalmologist to examine your eyes and give you glasses that fit your needs. When Roger was looking for leadership lenses, he discovered John Maxwell's *The 21 Irrefutable Laws of Leadership* (1998a, 1998b) and *The 21 Most Powerful Minutes in a Leader's Day* (2000). The language of Maxwell's leadership laws allowed Roger to put a much-needed frame on his leadership lenses. As he looked at each challenge in this new way, it brought great clarity to his leadership. Roger actually made flash cards of the title of each law, listing their biblical character and subtitle about leadership. This may sound a little hokey, but he realized he had to build influence with the congregation. He was expected to administer the budget, keep the facility clean and operating, continue to grow the youth group, and help lead the staff; and he was not equipped to do all of that. He knew he had to grow or else the church would look for someone else to fill this role.

If you are not on a continuous learning curve that helps you see your ministry through leadership lenses, this is the first and most important choice. You may take a completely different pathway from Roger's to find lenses that fit you best; a mentoring relationship with your first chair, a peer group with other leaders, or training events can all help you develop a leader's perspective. But more than just learning, you need to apply these lessons in your leadership context.

Choice Two: Maximize Major Opportunities

In a typical week, much of our time is spent on routine activities. Certain things have to be done, week in and week out, to keep the organization moving forward. Less frequently, you have unique opportunities to do something that stretches you as a leader and that can have tremendous benefit for your congregation.

Roger knows that God has gifted and called him to preach, but this was not a primary responsibility in his role of associate pastor. Early in his tenure, however, our senior pastor gave him the privilege of filling the pulpit when he was out of town. Roger's wife, Julee, eventually began to call him the "Holiday Preacher." During those times, Roger would call out to God to propel him forward in his relationship with the church. He also prayed that his efforts would always point back and give glory to God. He looks back on those experiences as a pivotal time in his becoming a second chair leader, and he thanks God for answering every one of those prayers.

Your moment of opportunity may not come in a pulpit. It may not be in front of the entire congregation or organization. Your opportunity may come when an important decision needs to be made, or a new ministry initiative launched, or a voice of faith is required in a time of crisis. You may be able to see the opportunity coming, or it might sneak up with no warning. Be prepared to recognize and act on those unique moments that can shape you and set you apart as a second chair leader.

Choice Three: Don't Back Down from the Right Decision

Sometimes a major leadership opportunity comes our way and we are tempted to run. The choice that a second chair must make is to pray first for God's wisdom, and then to make the right decision, even if it is not easy.

One of the toughest seasons in our team's leadership journey was in the spring and summer of 2000. We easily lived through "Y2K," but we barely survived the challenge of implementing a contemporary service. Several factors seemed to indicate the time was right to add a new worship service with a style different from our traditional format. We were growing, some of our new and younger families were asking for a new option, and our community demographics pointed in this direction. On paper, the decision was an easy one. The leadership challenge of pulling it off proved to be much harder.

We began the decision-making process early in the year, and by late summer we had two unsuccessful experiments to show for our efforts. More people were dissatisfied than when we started. The right answer seemed to be escaping us, and we were just a few months away from beginning a major capital campaign for a much-needed, campuswide renovation project. It looked like a leadership train wreck waiting to happen.

The last Sunday in August, our senior pastor announced we would be starting a contemporary service in mid-September. The following weekend was Labor Day, so guess who was asked to preach? Roger, the holiday preacher! As he began to prepare for this critical Sunday, Roger thought that a whirling rendition of "we can do it together with faith" would be an inspiring message. That week, however, the Lord shifted his focus to 1 Corinthians 12 and 13, concerning the body of Christ and our conduct with one another. His message that day was entitled, "Love Never Fails." God led Roger to speak truthfully about the two sets of opinions in the church and the division they were creating.

Roger was gripped by fear that day, not out of concern about the congregation's reaction but because of the mandate that God had put on his heart. At the end of his message, he tearfully told the congregation, "I am not your pastor, and I did not want to speak this message to you. But the Lord won't allow me to share anything else. We must apply this truth to our life and from this day forward live out the biblical mandate of loving each other." God used it as a healing time, as some of the most vocal and influential people from both sides thanked him for his willingness to speak a hard word from the Lord.

The point of this story is to focus not on Roger but on the fact that second chair leaders are called upon to follow God in some hard decisions and challenging moments. It is imperative that you walk confidently in the Lord and ask Him to give you favor with your congregation and constituents. When you ask, it is critical that you act in confidence that He is going to grant this favor. Only then are you inspired and confident in making the difficult, right leadership decisions of the second chair. Sometimes you may feel that the role requires more than you are willing to give. Leading in the second chair is very uncomfortable at times. It is challenging, and painful. It is not the most comfortable chair in the room, and it never will be. But when God comes through, you will experience a great sense of victory.

Choice Four: Decide to Thrive

Some people thrive in the second chair. Others only survive. The latter are constantly looking for a ticket to something better—a new set of duties, a better group of people to lead, a new boss. Those who thrive do so even in difficult circumstances. The difference, and the focus of this final choice, is attitude.

An essential attitude in the second chair is *submission*. This is recognition of the authority God has placed over your life; it calls you to submit willingly to that authority. Andy Stanley teaches Matthew 8:5–13 to make this point. In this Scripture passage, a Roman centurion asks Jesus to heal his servant. The centurion states, "But just say the word, and my servant will be healed. For I myself am a man under authority." Stanley (2002)

notes that the centurion saw that Jesus' authority was based on His submission to God's ultimate authority. An attitude of submission is not a
loss of authority. It is recognition of the source of authority. If you are to
model Christ to the world and to those in your ministry setting, you must
be willing to be under the authority that God has established. It is para-
mount that you possess this attitude of a submissive heart.

A related attitude is that of *service*. Possessing a servant's heart is
important, but what does that look like when you are also a leader? When
Roger waited tables in college, he saw waiters who knew how to truly
serve their guests and made a lot of money as a result. What he could not
understand was why other waiters did not offer the same excellent service. They did not seem to realize that each patron in their section repre-
sented a paycheck for the night. In truth, they did not want to serve. They
wanted the benefit of the fast and substantial cash each night, but they
did not have servants' hearts. Second chair leaders face the same question.
They often want the influence of the second chair but lack the willingness
to serve in order to receive it. When there is a crisis or a need within the
team, do you have an attitude of service? When you are asked to do something that is not in line with your agenda, gifts, or calling, are you glad to
help or annoyed? Do you have a "whatever it takes" attitude? If you truly
know how to serve, you understand there will be times when you are
inconvenienced for the sake of the organization. As a second chair leader,
you should always keep a servant's towel over your arm.

Are you *thankful* for your church, your senior leader, and the opportunities you have to serve and lead? Second chairs need to be "thankful in all circumstances" (1 Thessalonians 5:18). They should find
satisfaction in their current position in the organization for this season of
life. This is a hard choice because society teaches you to always want
more, never be satisfied, and constantly compare yourself with your peers.
When someone else receives a promotion or recognition, you should be
excited for them, not resentful. A positive, thankful attitude is a key factor determining whether you are effective in your ministry over a long
period of time.

The final attitude is a *passion* for being the best. This attitude causes
you to push back, ask questions, and challenge the thinking of others. It
challenges the other team members to pull their weight and be responsible as they carry out their duties. It is the other side of the coin that keeps
submission from being spineless. It is a counterbalance that keeps thank-
fulness from becoming carefree. It calls for excellence in the midst of contentment. You can have the other three attitudes and be a good second
chair leader; an attitude of passion distinguishes you as one of the best.

It is hard to discuss attitudes without reflecting on Paul's words in Philippians 2:5. He instructs that "your attitude should be the same as that of Christ Jesus" and goes on to paint a beautiful and powerful picture of our Lord's humility, servanthood, obedience, and determination. In the second chair, many people are watching to see what attitudes are modeled. We hope you will choose to practice each of these attitudes as you move forward in the adventure of second chair leadership.

SUBORDINATE-LEADER

THE SUBORDINATE-LEADER PARADOX is challenging to successfully balance because it is relationally intensive and partially dependent on another person: your first chair. It deals with how you as a leader are interfacing with and following the lead of your senior leader. Some first chairs are a pleasure to work with, and some are not. Some are concerned about the personal lives and careers of their subordinates, and others seem detached or self-absorbed. Some give their second chairs ample room to lead while others are much more controlling. At the end of the day, the second chair can do little to change the first chair. A second chair leader's most valuable tool for promoting change is his or her own attitudes and actions.

This does not mean that the second chair is to be a mindless robot, obeying whatever commands the first chair issues. Second chairs are leaders. Our definition makes it clear they are not content to sit back and wait for someone else to take action. This is the tension of the paradox. It is not easy to be a subordinate and a leader. We recognize that some circumstances may not allow a second chair to lead at all. As we discuss in Chapter Ten, some situations call for leaving your chair. But in most circumstances, you can discover the genius of the *and* as a subordinate *and* a leader.

Joseph did not start life as a master of the subordinate-leader paradox, but he apparently learned along the way. In a culture where age mattered a great deal, the way Joseph announced his dreams to his brothers and father was brash and disrespectful (Genesis 37:5–11). In short, he was insubordinate. He may have had natural leadership ability, painting a clear (and accurate) picture of God's plans for the future, but he did not understand the dynamics of second chair leadership. Like many immature or frustrated leaders, he said what was on his mind.

Two chapters and several years later in Joseph's life, the picture was quite different. After arriving in Egypt as a slave, Joseph quickly rose to a prominent position in Potiphar's house: "With Joseph in charge, he [Potiphar] did not concern himself with anything except the food he ate" (Genesis 39:6). Joseph had clearly earned Potiphar's trust. Somehow his talent and determination were visible enough for Potiphar to notice. Joseph must have continued to display leadership abilities to have been placed in this significant position over all the other servants in the household. Despite this quick rise to prominence, he must have also become more adept at subordination. An insubordinate slave would be in a grave, not in a place of authority.

Joseph had another tempting opportunity to be insubordinate, and this time he passed the test. "And after a while his master's wife took notice of Joseph and said, 'Come to bed with me!'" (Genesis 39:7). Joseph resisted the temptation repeatedly as she pursued him day after day. Joseph's response shows a much more complete understanding of the subordinate-leader paradox: "With me in charge . . . my master does not concern himself with anything in the house; everything he owns he has entrusted to my care. No one is greater in this house than I am" (Genesis 39:8).

Because Joseph feared God (v. 9) and had respect for the authority that God placed in his life, he was faithful. He chose loyalty over momentary pleasure or temporary power. He knew his role, and he chose not to cross over the line into insubordination. Because this was his heart, he could lead in the second chair.

Are you confident enough in God to realize He is using your first chair leader to further grow and develop you for His purposes in your life? Our desire is to help you understand the many facets of leadership in a subordinate role. With this understanding and confidence in God's hand in your life, your relationship with your first chair can be renewed. You can experience great fulfillment as a subordinate and leader as you thrive in the second chair.

3

TAKING IT FROM THE TOP

DO YOU FEEL EFFECTIVE in your current role as a second chair leader? Whether you answer yes or no, your relationship with your first chair is a key part of the response. If the relationship is healthy, most second chairs find a sense of freedom and fulfillment in their job, irrespective of the responsibilities assigned to them. But if ongoing tension or detachment characterizes the relationship, it is difficult to feel successful, even while the organization is flourishing. This is why anyone who aspires to realize his or her full potential as a second chair leader must start at the top—the top relationship, that is.

Warren Schuh knows a lot about second chair leadership. He is the executive pastor at Calvary Community Church in Westlake Village, California, and has also served as executive pastor of Mission Hills Church in Littleton, Colorado. In between these two local church roles, he served full-time as the coordinator of Leadership Network's Large Church Network, where he worked directly with executive pastors.

Warren's experience has taught him that the relationship with the first chair is critical for the second chair to function effectively: "Anyone in this role must come to grips with the subordinate-leader paradox." He considers the partnership between senior pastor and executive pastor to be similar to a marriage. A harmonious relationship is never guaranteed; it takes effort to make it work. These two leaders are often attracted by the other's opposite strengths because they recognize the value of complementary skills. But these differences can sow the seeds of conflict. Complementary strengths can pull in opposing and divisive directions if the relationship is not cultivated. The interaction between first and second chairs is fluid; it does not lend itself to a static job description.

Just like a marriage, great things can happen when first and second chair leaders work together in a close, harmonious relationship fueled by a unified vision of God's purpose for their ministry. The importance of this strong, healthy relationship is not unique to those who have the title of executive pastor. It is needed by anyone who fits our definition of a second chair leader. This chapter specifically addresses your relationship to your first chair. Second chair leaders who want to have the freedom to lead start by investing in this relationship. We look at the biblical concept of subordination to authority, define what subordination is and is not, and seek to understand key aspects of a healthy subordinate relationship.

A Biblical Standard

Are you willing to be subordinate? The question is more than a reflection on your relationship with your first chair. It is a question of spirit. J. Oswald Sanders's classic book *Spiritual Leadership* (1980) has much to say on this subject. Sanders challenges all leaders to have a Christ-like spirit of humility that puts others first. He also challenges leaders to learn to follow. Assess your willingness to be subordinate. Ask the Holy Spirit to reveal the degree to which your leadership is characterized by these three statements from Sanders's book:

 o Many who aspire to leadership fail because they have never learned to follow.

  o "Full of wisdom" was one of the requirements for even subordinate leaders in the early church (Acts 6:3).

o The spiritual leader of today is the one who gladly works as an assistant and associate, humbly helping another achieve great things [pp. 52, 57–58, 62].

What do you discover? Can you say that you fulfill these three requirements of leadership? Have you learned to follow? Do people look to you as one who is "full of wisdom"? Are you glad to work as an assistant, an associate? What are you helping another achieve? Sanders's insights cut to the heart of the subordinate-leader paradox because they call us to the place of subordination first and foremost.

A Call to Discipleship

A common denominator in these three statements is the thread of discipleship. This involves growing in your spiritual life and growing in your ability to follow. The disciples of Jesus' day were called by this name because they were followers. They followed Jesus everywhere He went. They followed His teaching and way of life. Effective second chair leaders are successful in the subordinate-leader paradox because they learn to follow and repeatedly choose to follow. Tom Billings says, "If a leader can't be a follower, he can't be an effective leader." Kim Miller's comment was similar: "Great leaders are ultimately great followers."

Learning is another important aspect of discipleship. Sanders challenges leaders to read and to constantly engage in learning opportunities for their own growth. In the first two of Sanders's statements, he brings this quality to light. He emphasizes the discipline of learning to follow and the character trait of being full of wisdom. The two go hand-in-hand; you cannot have one without the other. But you can possess both if you have a teachable spirit, which is critical to success in the subordinate-leader paradox. Leaders with a teachable spirit are willing to acknowledge their mistakes and seek wise counsel because they know this is the best way to learn.

Ultimately, second chair leaders should desire that people see them as full of wisdom. They cannot possess this trait unless they learn to follow. We have learned that God placed our first chair leader, Barry Landrum, in our lives so that we might learn from his leadership and experience. In learning to follow, we have discovered that our ways are not always right and that our solutions are not always best. We have been given uncomfortable and challenging assignments; each experience has added to our wisdom. If we did not have teachable spirits, we would miss great opportunities to learn and grow as followers and leaders.

Sanders also emphasizes the importance of a spirit of humility. Leaders must be willing to serve; they should not consider any task to be beneath them. As you serve in the second chair, do you do so gladly and humbly? The direct application of Sanders's teaching is in how we relate to peers. But humility is also essential in the relationship between second chair and leader. Anyone who lacks humility is certain to encounter conflict with the first chair.

A Higher Calling

Is any calling higher than to be a leader in an important ministry that is making a difference in your community? Do you remember what Jesus said? He made it very clear when the mother of James and John approached Him to secure their position in the coming Kingdom. Look at Christ's response: "You know that the rulers of the Gentiles lord it over them, and their high officials exercise authority over them. Not so with you. Instead, whoever wants to become great among you must be your servant, and whoever wants to be first must be your slave—just as the Son of Man did not come to be served, but to serve, and to give his life as a ransom for many" (Matthew 20:25–28).

Jesus taught that leadership in His Kingdom involves subordination. Leadership is not about position, title, or the role we want to play. For those who claim to love and follow Jesus, leading in His Kingdom involves service, subordination, and even slavery.

For Roger, the biblical standard of subordination was a challenge because God wired him to be a first chair leader someday. One big step in his growth was learning that he could enjoy the journey even if things were not exactly as he wanted. For a season, he was discontent and frustrated. His sister described him as a restless tiger pacing back and forth in his cage. But God taught Roger a great deal, and he has come to the place of gladly serving in his current role. Through God's love, patience, and sanctifying work, Roger was molded and shaped for a purpose during this season. The immediate purpose is the privilege of humbly and graciously partnering with a superb leader and leadership team to achieve great things in the heart of Houston. The long-term purpose is something he knows God will reveal in the future.

If you live and lead according to the biblical standard, you honor God, strengthen your congregation, and more ably serve those whom God has placed in the lead position in His church. Whether God is ultimately preparing you for a first chair role or a lifetime of service in the second chair, you are much better equipped for the future because of your growth as a faithful disciple.

What Is Subordination?

As we developed the material for this book, we struggled with the right label for this paradox. For most leaders, subordination is not an appealing word. In one sense, being subordinate is the opposite of exercising leadership. Yet our contention is that effective second chair leaders practice subordination *and* leadership. So, what is subordination?

Characteristics of Subordination

Subordination is recognizing and accepting that you are not the lead leader. It is acknowledging that you do not have the final authority; nor do you have the ultimate responsibility. The second chairs we interviewed expressed this in a variety of ways. Tom Billings never really felt he was

it's more than this – cf. biblical theme of submission

a subordinate, but when Union Baptist Association experienced a crisis in 1994 Tom knew that Executive Director Jim Herrington was the one on the firing line. Glenn Smith was very aware that the "senior pastor has a shirt with concentric circles and is always being shot at." Kelli Caskey, who shares the title of copastor with her husband, often responds to an issue by saying, "These are my views, but Guy [her husband] should be the one to decide."

Subordination, however, is more than recognition and acceptance. It brings in an attitude of serving with humility and gladness. Do you possess a genuine servant's attitude? One second chair described watching her first chair give a major presentation she had prepared. She could have sought credit when he received the accolades, but she recognized that this would only undermine him. Instead, she found satisfaction in having done her job well. Geoff Surratt acknowledges it can be difficult to not receive credit for an idea he developed. But he has learned that allowing the first chair to have credit for an idea "is not an ego thing for the senior pastor; it's what is needed to work most effectively."

Subordination requires a spirit of loyalty that is expressed in your conversation and action. Preston Mitchell, of Fellowship Church in Dallas, says, "Loyalty is the key. Loyalty is the number one characteristic to build staff and a great support team." What happens when you disagree with your first chair? Loyalty is displayed by a tame tongue in public and a practice of dealing with those disagreements in private. Warren Schuh says it simply: "Make up your mind you're not going to express resentment to anyone else." Loyalty also involves taking the heat in place of your first chair. Preston also says, "As a second chair, I must be willing to take shots publicly and cover his back. It is my job to protect Ed [the senior pastor] from the dirty stuff."

Subordination grows out of reverence for God. The second chair leader understands that God is the ultimate authority, and the giver of authority. Dan Reiland states that "all authority is transferred, first from God to the senior pastor, then from the senior pastor to the other pastoral staff." Gary Ferbet describes having a clear sense of his authority coming from beyond himself. In recognizing that God is the source of all authority and that He transfers it as He chooses, a successful second chair leader walks reverently before God. One way Gary does this is by serving the human authority that has been placed in his life.

We often talk about God calling us to a specific place of ministry. The second chair leaders we interviewed believed just as strongly that God uniquely called their first chair into the specific role. Geoff Surratt, of Seacoast Church, says, "This is God's ministry and it's also Greg's [the senior pastor's] party. If I'm not happy with this party, I need to figure out what's going on in me or go to a different party." Ric Hodgin, in talking about the major changes in the future for the A.D. Players (a Christian theater group), says, "I believe that she [the first chair] is going to be here. And I believe that I'm going to be here." Ric's comment expresses a clear belief that he and the first chair he serves are both called by God into their respective roles. When you have this belief about the lead leader, it sheds a different light on the issue of subordination.

Some second chair leaders see their subordinate role as a season in their career before they move into a first chair position. This long-term calling does not negate the importance of being subordinate while serving as second chair. Tom Billings was a senior pastor before coming to Union Baptist Association in a second chair role, and he has ultimately moved into the first chair role in the organization. Of his time in the second chair, Tom reflects, "I realized that my role was to be supportive of Jim [the first chair]." This is a very different attitude from that of a second chair who says, "I'm here to get my ticket punched. I hope my work will be noticed so that I can move on to the next, more significant role."

Other second chairs know that a first chair role is not in their future. This may make it easier for them to accept the tensions of the position. Kim Miller says, "I'd last about three days if I had to call the shots by myself. I like not being absolutely on top." Preston Mitchell's thoughts were similar: "I have no desire to be in Ed's [the first chair's] position."

Testing Your Subordination

Whether you see yourself as a second chair for life or a first chair in training, whether your role is vocational or volunteer, you will have experiences and seasons in which subordination does not come easily. It is hard to know how you are doing in this area until some kind of conflict arises. You might assess your own attitude toward subordination by testing your "subordination quotient." How do you respond when the first chair does something you dislike? Take a look at these brief scenarios and reflect on how you most likely would respond:

o When your first chair goes against your recommendation on a
   particular decision

o When your first chair criticizes a decision you have made or an
   action you have taken

o When your first chair gives someone else an important job you
   think you should do

Rate yourself on each question using this scale:

> 1 = *Fight*: you openly disagree and directly challenge your first chair.
>
> 2 = *Flight*: you walk away wounded and feel like giving up.
>
> 3 = *Stay involved without confrontation*: you accept the decision for what it is but stay engaged in the discussion and accept the first chair's final decision, whatever it may be.

[handwritten margin note: not the only 3 options! inadequate view of conflict / disagreement]

This third option may be the most difficult to define, and it is certainly the most difficult to carry out. You may still disagree with the decision, but you understand when the decision is final. You assume the best of the first chair. You talk directly with him about your feelings and frustrations if the matter is significant enough to you.

How did you do? We each have a mixture of the three responses, but we also have a tendency toward one of them. Even though this is not a scientific survey, the conclusion is clear. A lower rating indicates a greater tendency to engage in some form of insubordinate behavior. A higher rating suggests you are better at handling the inevitable tensions of the relationship with your first chair. Subordination does not mean giving up; it means staying engaged and working through differences while accepting the ultimate leadership role of the first chair in the organization.

Notice in this simple test that a second chair leader who is subordinate is still highly involved in the leadership process; he or she is not a doormat and does not listen to the first chair with a resigned, whatever-you-say attitude. The second chair is vocal in expressing ideas for improving his or her ministry and wants to fully use his or her spiritual gifts. Being deeply involved and not being insubordinate, even in disagreement, is the tension of the role.

Some actions and attitudes are clearly inconsistent with the practice of being subordinate. First, subordination is not self-serving. Leaders should not look for their own glory. Their language should use an inclusive *we* rather than a self-promoting *I* whenever possible. They should put the organization first and themselves second. Sometimes this means staying out of the spotlight to clear the way for the first chair. When they are in a more visible position, effective second chairs give praise to God, respect to their leaders, and credit to those who have assisted them.

Subordination is not power-hungry. Second chair leaders should use their influence and gifts to support the first chair. They should never work for leadership approval and acceptance by people in a way that opposes the lead leader. When asked about his relationship with his senior pastor,

[handwritten note at bottom: people of God first!]

Gary Ferbet responded that he is careful to avoid any actions that could be construed as competitive or divisive. A previous experience as a copastor ended in significant conflict, teaching Gary the importance of unity among key leaders. Likewise, the second chair should not withhold information from the senior leader. A good second chair leader gives the first chair all of the information necessary to make well-informed decisions.

Subordination is not offensive in communication. This involves your words and your body language. Are you careful in what you say and when you say it? Do you know how much you say to the first chair and to others in the room even while you are not talking? The timing and tone of your comments matter almost as much as your actual words. Anything spoken in confidence must stay that way. Your facial expression and simple gestures speak volumes. Your communication should always be circumspect.

things above all apply to 1st chair too.

The Right Relationship

If you want to succeed as a second chair leader, the key lesson of this chapter is, "The right relationship is everything!" You may know that the relationship with your first chair is important, but do your actions and attitude demonstrate your belief in this statement? Honestly ask yourself, "Would I rather have the right answer, or the right relationship?" This simple question often confuses second chair leaders. They do not believe they should have to choose. Why should taking a firm position for a well-researched answer be the cause of any relational damage? In an ideal world, you do not have to make this choice. But in the real world of human frailty, egos, and miscommunication, this trade-off is common.

As a second chair leader, you often have more information on a subject than your first chair does. Sometimes you can make an independent decision on the basis of your knowledge. At other times, your role is to furnish information so that your first chair can make a wise leadership decision. In this capacity, you are a knowledgeable advisor but not the ultimate decision maker. You often have definite opinions about the right answer, but your leader may make a decision with which you disagree. If you know in your heart that your way is better, what should you do? After you have clearly explained your recommendation, how do you respond if your first chair chooses a different solution? Is it better to insist on the supposed right decision, even if doing so compromises the relationship with your first chair? Or should you offer your best counsel and defer on the final decision in order to preserve a strong relationship?

These issues often involve minor decisions that you are responsible for implementing. You can push back and strive to go in another direction.

leadership principle: hold your ideas loosely

Because you have more information, you may persuade your first chair to reluctantly accept your recommendation. But are you displaying loyalty and a right relationship in these minor situations? If not, you may be tempted to say, "It's just a small issue." In truth, the behavior patterns and level of trust established in these day-to-day encounters spill over into the big decisions. The price of winning a small battle may be that you are pushed to the margin or even excluded from more strategic issues.

Glenn Smith learned the lesson of right relationship in a pivotal way early in his tenure as executive pastor of Sugar Creek Baptist. He was uncomfortable with the way his senior pastor, Fenton Moorhead, dealt with a staff member in a meeting. After reflecting on how to handle the situation, Glenn decided to write Fenton a memo outlining his concern. He spent considerable time writing and rewriting, trying to make his point clear without being insubordinate. When Fenton got the memo, he asked Glenn to come and discuss it, and they agreed on a course of action. Then Fenton asked Glenn never to do it again; if he had a concern, he should raise it in person. This event actually led to weekly meetings between Glenn and Fenton that greatly strengthened their relationship.

Any second chair will feel tension in the subordinate-leader paradox, so it is important not to let the tension drive a wedge into the relationship. Ric Hodgin consistently invests in his relationship with Jeannette Clift George, the A.D. Players' founder and artistic director. Ric has done many things, personally and professionally, to keep his relationship with Jeannette strong. Rather than blaming his first chair when tensions arise, as many second chairs are inclined to do, Ric looks first to himself as the potential source of problems. This does not mean that a first chair is always right or a second chair always wrong, but Ric's attitude gives this crucial relationship a much stronger footing.

Would you rather be right on the issues, or in right relationship? As you seek to be in right relationship first and foremost, you are more successful in implementing your approach to ministry. You cultivate credible and lasting influence with your senior leader. You will influence the organization over the long haul because of the relational seeds you sow. A right relationship opens the door for success in the second chair.

A Foundation of Trust

A variety of characteristics are important for a person to be successful in any ministry or leadership role. Competence, good interpersonal skills, dependability, integrity, and commitment are all necessary. For second chair leaders, however, the attribute at the top of the list is trust. Just as

Potiphar entrusted Joseph with everything in his house, second chair leaders need to earn the full trust of their leaders. Trust is more than a characteristic; it is the foundation for an effective partnership between first and second chair. Many benefits can be realized by a second chair who is trusted by the first chair. If you have not reached that position of full trust, do not give up. Look for signs that the level of trust in the relationship is expanding. Reaching a level of complete trust requires faithful service, but more than that it requires patience over a long period of time.

As Glenn Smith partnered with Fenton Moorhead, Sugar Creek experienced substantial growth of its own and planted thirty-six congregations. These new works reached seven thousand additional people over and above those attending Sugar Creek. What was the secret of their partnership? Did they just have great chemistry from day one? Glenn had learned the importance of building trust when he held a similar position in a prior church. He also knew that earning trust takes time, and he was willing to be patient with the process. He says, "I was executive pastor in title only, initially. It was three years before I had the trust and freedom to do the job."

Greg Hawkins, executive pastor at Willow Creek Community Church, had a similar experience. Even though he was promoted into his second chair role from within the organization, this did not guarantee him carte blanche when it came to trust. In reality, there are many levels of trust. He started in his role with a threshold level of trust, and it grew over time. Greg estimates that Bill Hybels's trust of him was not fully developed until four years after he became executive pastor.

What allowed these and other second chair leaders to earn their senior leader's highest level of trust? Obviously, they chose to be in right relationship and were willing to be subordinate. They understood the boundaries for their role, which is the focus of the next chapter. But they did more than just stay out of trouble or play it safe.

Second chair leaders need to be bold. They need to make a difference in their organization. They must be trusted with large, organization-shaping responsibilities: leading a church planting movement (Glenn Smith, Sugar Creek), developing a strategic planning process and overhauling the small-group ministry (Greg Hawkins, Willow Creek), creating a multisite network of churches (Geoff Surratt, Seacoast Church), overseeing all creative productions and communications (Kim Miller, Ginghamsburg Church). These are organizationwide, critical assignments entrusted to second chair leaders. How did they earn the trust?

Chemistry between the two leaders is an important factor. Glenn Smith said, "The senior leader and the second chair need to be two sides of the same coin." The majority of the second chair leaders we interviewed saw their gifts and skills as different from and highly complementary to those of their first chair. When this happens, the second chair has the potential to add great value to the work being done by the senior leader. The importance of complementary skills means that second chairs are not interchangeable parts. The abilities that make someone an ideal executive pastor for one senior pastor may cause conflict with another. Greg Hawkins says quite simply, "I have no illusions that I'd be the right person with a different senior pastor."

With these complementary skills comes a feeling of mutual respect. A second chair who does the job well earns the respect of the first chair. But the second chair needs to have a high level of respect for the first chair as a leader. Absence of respect sows the seeds of discontent and insubordination. Kim Miller laughed about some of her senior pastor's weaknesses but quickly added that she had always been able to follow him because of his integrity and strong spiritual leadership.

Interestingly, complementary skills and mutual respect do not inherently mean that first and second chairs are good friends socially. Several second chairs described a great working relationship with their first chair but relatively little that drew them together outside of work. Greg Hawkins said that he and Bill Hybels have little natural affinity: "Bill loves to sail; I get seasick. Bill thinks eating is a utility function; I'm an aspiring gourmet. He's from Michigan; I'm from Texas."

They may not have a natural affinity, but the successful pairs make up for it with common vision and passion. Geoff Surratt says, "Be 100 percent sure that you know the senior pastor's vision and are totally committed to it." Kim Miller said that her vision aligns so closely with Senior Pastor Mike Slaughter's that it "sustains me on the most annoying of days." Glenn Smith and Fenton Moorhead were both passionate about the church planting movement they launched at Sugar Creek.

A final trust builder is time. We have already talked about the time that was required for Glenn Smith and Greg Hawkins to reach a high level of trust in the eyes of their senior pastors. If you are not prepared to be patient while trust grows, you are unlikely to reach your full potential as a second chair leader. You simply cannot rush the process. Warren Schuh offered another marriage analogy when he described the early stages of the relationship between first and second chair: "It is like someone who has been married less than a year. If they tell you they have it all figured out, that's when you should really worry." The role of second chair, regardless of the specific title, has far too many nuances for someone to step into the job and understand all the subtleties from the very beginning.

(this means you will fail?)

Even at the highest level of trust, there are challenges. Geoff Surratt has a great working relationship with his brother, Senior Pastor Greg Surratt, but Geoff also gets frustrated by the 5 percent of his decisions that Greg overrides. As you work closely with your first chair, moments of frustration, friction, and tension are unavoidable. The stories of Glenn Smith and others show that you can earn trust and accomplish great things in God's Kingdom in the second chair. Look for progress in various aspects of your relationship with your first chair. Think about your relationship with your first chair in the areas of communication, affirmation, and congregational influence. You may be on the verge of realizing the trust that has taken so long to build. If not, you may begin to see how you can become a trust builder.

The Benefits of a Right Relationship

When your relationship with your first chair is based on trust and your gifts complement each other, you experience many benefits. More important, it benefits the Kingdom cause that you seek to advance. So what are the benefits you can expect to realize?

An open line of communication is one of the first things you might experience as the trust relationship begins to blossom. If your first chair has confidence in your ability and trusts you to work for the good, not for harm, communication will flow freely. Communication is one of those intangible qualities with huge benefits in your work. When it is deficient, you feel isolated and left out of important decisions. When communication is open, you feel the privilege of being in the middle of the game. As this happens, you grow and add value. You better understand the leadership burdens that the first chair is experiencing. Communication is both a benefit and an essential element for a second chair who wants to build and maintain a healthy relationship with the first chair.

The personal benefits of a right relationship go far beyond improved communication. Think about a time when you had a positive working relationship with your immediate supervisor. The relationship probably made the entire work environment more relaxed and enjoyable. You found more satisfaction in your job and were more productive. In fact, you probably had opportunities to take on new challenges. At the end of the day, you did not feel as though you were carrying a fifty-pound bag of stress home.

The benefits are not limited to you and your first chair. As the level of trust and communication increases, the entire team becomes more unified. The relationship between first and second chairs is not a private matter.

Other team members can tell when the relationships at the top are strong and when they are fragile. If these key relationships are right, those who follow are strengthened. They are more encouraged to do their part. They are not forced to choose sides or wonder about their future. A unified team yields great dividends for the ministry.

Strong, trust-based relationships flourish in an environment in which honesty and integrity are valued in making decisions. Even though this may not describe your current organization, you can work toward this standard. As second chair, you long for the opportunity to speak frankly about a matter to your first chair and then see the counsel followed. You want your organization to perform at its very best. In fact, honest and open decision making is not the end goal; it is a means to improve your ministry's effectiveness. Dena Harrison began serving in a second chair role at the diocesan level under Bishop Claude Payne, a capable leader whose gifts were quite different from hers. Nevertheless, they developed a profound respect for each other. In fact, their differences, and Dena's ability to offer honest input, were the key to their strong working relationship.

Ultimately, the benefit of being in a right relationship with your senior leader is the opportunity to see your ministry soar to the next level. A congregation appreciates harmony between the second chairs and first chair. Its members want to see the staff and pastor on the same page as God works out His purposes in their midst. The congregation's buy-in and contribution to the ministry always increase when this occurs. As more people contribute their time and talents, ministry effectiveness grows exponentially. Your influence also increases because you are given additional opportunities to serve. In a trust-based relationship between the two chairs, the first chair looks to the second chair to shape key decisions and to fill key roles. Most second chairs thrive on the challenge of being the go-to person when the stakes are high, the person who is known for getting the job done. They take great satisfaction in knowing they have added value throughout the organization. They understand that this is only possible in the context of their relationship at the top.

The Consequences of a Wrong Relationship

How does your first chair perceive you? Are you seen as loyal, trustworthy, and competent? Or might you be perceived as insubordinate, opportunistic, or self-serving? You may be striving to implement all the principles found in this book, but if you are perceived to be out for your own interests you will not be successful in the second chair. This perception could be caused by your actions or by your first chair's insecurity. It could be based on recent events or something in the distant past. What-ever the reason, your first chair's perception ultimately shapes your reality. This is what happened to the relationship between Joseph and Potiphar. Potiphar perceived that Joseph tried to take something away from him, and Joseph wound up in a dungeon. For most second chairs, neither the issues nor the results are this severe, but the principle is the same. If your first chair has a negative perception, you may experience consequences, whether warranted or not. The second chair needs to work overtime to avoid spiraling downward relationally.

A frequent consequence of a first chair's loss of confidence is micro-management. In times of stress, a senior leader may display misgivings or insecurity by giving staff members less freedom to act and becoming more involved in their decisions. If you find you are being kept on a tighter rein, step away and examine the situations in which this is happening. Can you find a common thread, or a recent trust buster? You may need to sit down and ask your leader about your relationship: "Have I done something to cause you to lose confidence or trust in me?" Be ready for whatever answer you receive. Maturing in the second chair requires willingness to reflect, take note, and change your own behavior when necessary.

Some first chairs micromanage when relations are strained; others avoid their second chairs altogether. Some leaders find it hard to confront per-formance issues they see in their staff. They may perceive a staff member as unable or unwilling to change. As a result, they might choose to com-pletely bypass the person or the situation. If you sense this happening, be proactive and humbly ask for feedback. In doing so, you are giving your leader permission to speak into your life. Again, you must possess a teach-able spirit and a willingness to grow. Listen carefully, but do not respond defensively. Being defensive simply confirms that you really do not want to grow or change, thereby confirming the negative image of you. If you have an open heart and mind and if you address the issues that are raised, you just may be able to reverse the perception.

If the ultimate benefit of a right relationship is growing influence, the ultimate consequence of a wrong relationship is lost influence and lost opportunity. The best way to counteract this is to be sensitive to the rela-tionship and remedy any problems quickly. We rarely have confrontations with our senior pastor, but when we do we take it upon ourselves to go to him and make sure we are in a right relationship. Once, at the Willow Creek Leadership Summit, Roger heard Bill Hybels use the expression, "Are we good?" For Hybels and his staff, this phrase begins the process of reconciliation. This simple question, if asked in sincerity, quickly and certainly moves hearts back toward one another instead of allowing them to stay divided. You, as a second chair, have the responsibility to take this initiative instead of waiting on your first chair to make a move.

A Final Tip

If you want to learn to be a second chair leader, pay particular attention to the waitstaff the next time you go to a restaurant. You may think, "A waiter isn't a leader." Maybe, but you can learn some valuable lessons in the experience.

Waiters truly are servants. They have no say in who their clientele are and little control over how much they are paid. They try to offer superb service because of the potential for a good income in tips each night. When Roger first began waiting tables, it was all he could do to keep everyone's order straight and keep the customers happy. Eventually he was able to anticipate the needs of his guests. Before they asked, Roger could serve a refill, clean the table, or produce a timely check. This required him to be available enough to offer great service and a great experience, though without the customers noticing him too much. Sometimes he became an annoyance by getting ahead of his guests. He wanted them to hurry and finish so he could turn the table and gain more business. Or he would try to take the plates off the table discreetly, not realizing that a talkative guest still had three or four bites left of an entree. He had to learn that great service is not a function of speed; it requires balance, attentiveness, and timing.

Leading from the second chair is like waiting tables. We must strive to give our senior leaders great service. Yet sometimes in haste, aggression, or inexperience, we run ahead of our first chair and become an annoyance—or worse. Instead of receiving excellent service, the first chair ends up washing dishes, so to speak, in some sort of damage control situation. As a subordinate, learn to take note of how your leader wants to be served. Strike the balance that allows you to excel in your service to your first chair and to the rest of the organization. Be the kind of waiter whose customers are delighted to reward with a large tip. Preston Mitchell said it well: "Every great leader has to have leaders supporting him or her. They can't do it alone." We must strive to be servant leaders, putting others' needs, wants, and desires ahead of our own.

The analogy of the waiter illustrates some important concepts, but it also breaks down in two ways. The difference between being a servant and a servant-leader is significant. Waiters are not called upon to lead. They are not trying to get others to follow; nor are they making bold decisions to improve their organization. A second chair who is only a servant does not help the organization reach its full potential.

[handwritten margin notes: "for the sake of X or the people" ; "this moves away from biblical language on being a servant"]

Waiters are not required to be leaders, and they are not in a long-term relationship with the customers. Some customers are impossible to please, regardless of the level of service received. The waiter's consolation is in probably never having to wait on those customers again. The second chair cannot solve the dilemma of a difficult first chair nearly as easily. Just like the challenging customer, some first chairs refuse to be satisfied. What should you do when your best is not good enough for a demanding or unreasonable leader? You will often be tempted to respond in anger or try to right the situation on your own. At times, the best answer may be to leave, a topic we explore in Chapter Ten. But as long as you remain in your current chair, you should endeavor to serve with excellence.

One final story, from the Diocese of Texas, captures the essence of this chapter. As Bishop Payne neared retirement and the diocese prepared to elect a new bishop, Dena Harrison and Don Wimberly were the two leading contenders. The two had served together for three years and held a strong mutual respect. In a conversation before the election, they agreed that neither wanted to lose the relationship over the election. After Wimberly was elected, he promoted Dena to the role of archdeacon and gave her considerable responsibility and authority. They continue to have a very positive working partnership that is grounded in their complementary gifts and healthy relationship. With first and second chair leaders in harmony, titles lose their significance and the Kingdom is advanced.

4

CROSSING THE LINE

YOU HAVE WORKED DILIGENTLY for several years to build a strong, trust-based relationship with your first chair. Now you get to reap the benefits. But this does not mean you can put the relationship on autopilot. Nor does it mean the remainder of your time together will be smooth sailing, free of any storms.

In the previous chapter, Warren Schuh described the relationship between first and second chair as analogous to a marriage. An absence of conflict is not what makes a marriage strong. A healthy marriage is one in which husband and wife have learned to manage conflict in appropriate, constructive ways. Similarly, the relationship between first chair and second chair will have points of conflict. Discord may be caused by personal clashes, unresolved issues from the past, or external factors that are divisive. Some disagreements may relate to differing visions (which is a subject for the third paradox). Another major cause of conflict is when the second chair crosses over an invisible line. Something said or done is perceived as overstepping authority, or even bordering on insubordination.

By our definition, second chairs are leaders. They want the best for the ministry. They are trying to understand the big picture and how significant decisions affect the entire church. They have specific ideas for improving the organization's effectiveness. They are willing to try new approaches that may help the congregation achieve its vision. This way of thinking and taking initiative is characteristic of leaders. A person who is truly a second chair, in deed and not just in title, thinks and behaves in this way. It is this independence and drive that can lead to problems. In short, when a well-meaning second chair takes initiative, he or she may unintentionally run counter to the desires of the lead leader.

When first and second chair leaders disagree, it is no small matter. Other disagreements in the organization may not be consequential, but a rift at the top cannot be ignored. Compare conflict between spouses with conflict between neighbors. Neighbors can use time and distance to allow the conflict to subside; spouses cannot avoid all the day-to-day parts of life and the constant interaction that comes with it. Resolving the conflict as quickly and positively as possible is critical for peace in the house. A pattern of ongoing conflict does not make for a good marriage. Likewise, senior leaders need to establish working relationships that are harmonious. They need to have healthy ways of resolving the differences that inevitably occur.

In many marriages, the spouses agree on some general ways of dividing household responsibilities: cooking, shopping, repairs, financial matters, yard work, and more. Rarely, however, is this division of work cast in concrete. Rather, think of each of these responsibilities being written on separate index cards and spread out on a table, with a piece of string dividing the cards into two halves. The string can be moved easily. Sometimes the string is moved for a day or two, when one spouse has a stressful day or is out of town. Sometimes it is moved for a longer period of time, in the event of serious illness (or when one spouse is writing a book!). Sometimes circumstances change, causing the line to be moved permanently, as when a job change occurs. Sometimes the actual cards change, as when a child is born, requiring that the line be redrawn to reflect a new division for a new set of responsibilities. Healthy, long-term relationships require three things: recognition of the existence of the line, flexibility in placement of the line, and caution in crossing the line.

One quite stressful time in our tenure as second chair leaders at West University Baptist illustrates our failure with all three of these requirements. It happened quite unexpectedly at a staff retreat. In the weeks immediately before the retreat, Barry Landrum, our senior pastor, voiced concern that our worship attendance was no longer growing. Since joining the staff, Mike had become the numbers guy, so he prepared the data and graphs on worship attendance for the retreat. On the first evening of our retreat, we experienced a powerful time of seeking God in prayer. We thanked Him for the many blessings we were experiencing at the church, and we asked Him to guide our time of planning. The question about worship attendance was just one of several agenda items the next day. When we came to that point in the discussion, Mike handed out his packet of information and explained that attendance was still growing. The trend line was flat for our traditional service, but it showed growth in our contemporary service. Barry looked at the same information and saw cause for concern; the ensuing discussion became heated at times. Barry was convinced we had a problem that needed to be addressed. Mike and Roger and some of our colleagues did not see the problem and were not enthusiastic about making the changes proposed by our first chair. By the time we finally agreed to disagree and implement some simple changes that Barry wanted, the positive spirit of the previous night was gone. The rest of the meeting was tense and perfunctory.

Back in the office the day after the retreat, Barry had a follow-up meeting with the two of us. He did not like the way we had disagreed with him, and he perceived that we were working against him. In essence, he felt we had been insubordinate. Even though we knew the retreat had ended on a sour note, we were quite surprised that Barry perceived us as standing in opposition to him. Fortunately, and providentially, Barry chose to voice these concerns. We both apologized for our actions and affirmed our commitment to follow his leadership. We assured him that we never intended to be insubordinate.

It took time to restore our relationships to full strength and trust again, but we both learned valuable lessons about crossing the line. Mike thought he had a clear understanding of the existence and location of the line that defined his role. He prepared the statistics and believed he was the unquestioned expert in their interpretation. He learned, though, that he did not have a monopoly on analyzing trends; the first chair could move the line in this respect. More important, Mike failed to recognize another line: the one relating to how to disagree with the first chair when others are involved in the discussion. As a result, he inadvertently crossed the line and exacerbated the situation by staying on the wrong side.

The theme of this chapter is really quite simple. First, recognize that a line exists. It defines responsibilities and authority, and it is much more than what is conveyed in a job description. Second, those who cross the line do so at their own peril. Crossing the line is insubordination, and the relationship between first and second chair cannot survive if insubordination exists. Third, it is possible to proactively move the line. It takes time and trust, but second chair roles can be reshaped. To bring it back full circle, many second chair leaders begin to have problems when they accidentally cross a line that they failed to recognize. Finding the lines that set your boundaries is a crucial part of the subordinate-leader paradox.

Finding the Line

The line defines your responsibilities—what you are expected to do, what you are authorized to do, and what is out of bounds. Do you have a clear idea of where the line is for you? Can you describe with certainty which decisions you can make without consulting your first chair, which require first chair approval, and which you should not even touch? If you are a second chair leader, this answer may not be found in a job description.

More Than a Job Description

In many ways, the responsibility boundary lines are hardest to define for someone who is a second chair and easier to specify for others in the organization. This can be illustrated by a "job description test." If a written job description accurately explains your role and how most of your time is spent, you may not be a second chair leader yet. If your job really begins with the last line of the position description ("and all other duties as assigned"), it points toward a second chair type of role. The second chairs we interviewed experienced great variety within their job, the kind that is not easily captured in a written job description. Of course, this test is just one indicator. Furthermore, roles can differ in the degree of second chair characteristics.

So where is the line? For second chair leaders, it is often dynamic. They have specific responsibilities, but much of their role is based on the needs and traits of the first chair and the current circumstances of the organization. Second chair leaders who do have a formal job description often find the words on the paper to be grossly inadequate or frustratingly restrictive. After all, the second chair wants the very best for the organization. How can anyone possibly write a job description that accurately includes all the actions that might be required to help the organization succeed?

Return to the question with which we began this section: How do you define the line? If not by a job description, how do you know what you should or should not, can or cannot do? All of the second chair leaders we interviewed had certain core responsibilities. The specifics varied, including things such as managing the staff, designing or leading the worship experience, and overseeing administrative functions. These tasks were usually only a portion of how they spent their time. Another portion was spent doing special assignments at the request of the first chair. This is often a significant part of the second chair's job.

But even these two categories do not encompass the full scope of a second chair's role. Think about how you define success in your role. Now think about how your first chair defines it. If you do all the specific activities in your job description (if you have one) plus any other duties that the first chair has assigned, will you be successful? In all likelihood, the answer is no. As a second chair leader, you expect—and are expected—to be an initiator. You are expected to see and act on things that help the organization function better. As Greg Hawkins says, "I don't wait for Bill (Hybels) to tell me to fix a problem."

This certainly makes it more difficult to define your role, which is exactly the point. How do you find the line? It begins with your relationship with your first chair leader. Even though this was the subject of the previous chapter, it merits further explanation here. You can have a strong, positive relationship with your first chair leader without having a clear idea of how you are expected to function in your role. You need to move beyond relational health to a working partnership. For example, you should have a clear idea of the first chair's strengths and weaknesses, and how your abilities might complement them. You must have an understanding of your first chair's thought processes. How does she process information when making decisions? What is the best way to provide the information she requires? Knowing her preferred communication style informs you of the best way to communicate. You must also know how much you are trusted. How much freedom do you have to launch a new initiative, or make organizational changes?

Glenn Smith learned this lesson the hard way in his initial second chair role. He was the successful youth pastor of a nondenominational church in Indiana, supervising five staff members and a ministry that was larger than that of many churches. He also had a great deal of autonomy in running this ministry. After five years on staff, the elders asked Glenn to move into the role of ministry director, a position similar to that of executive pastor and clearly defined as the number two position on the organization chart. The elders had seen Glenn's success in the youth ministry and wanted the same effectiveness in the other ministries of the church. Glenn naturally assumed that the new title and position also conveyed a commensurate level of authority.

He discovered that the new position was actually more restrictive than his role as youth pastor. He was now reporting to the senior pastor, an individual who was not a very strong leader and who was not comfortable with Glenn's promotion. The way Glenn took the reins in his new position did nothing to calm these fears: "I did not realize that I had to earn and manage trust" in the new role. In essence, he had already crossed an invisible line as far as his first chair was concerned. Glenn made decisions that appeared to be consistent with his position but that the senior pastor was not ready to release. Not surprisingly, Glenn was frustrated by the growing conflict over his role. He compounded his problems and crossed another invisible line when he confronted the senior pastor quite directly. It seemed reasonable to Glenn to discuss these issues openly and seek a resolution, but this approach further eroded the trust level. After three unhappy years, Glenn left the church, vowing never to be an executive pastor again.

Through intentional observation, you can learn much about your first chair's style and preferences. But this is not a substitute for good communication. If you are in doubt about the location of the line, ask for clarification. This is especially important when the relationship is still new or when the organization is undergoing significant changes. Asking for clearer role definition is a balancing act. If you are constantly seeking direction, your first chair may become frustrated; you may not be ready for second chair leadership yet. If you never ask for clarification, you are probably taking too many risks of crossing the line. Find the balance, and within it do not be afraid to ask. The longer you serve with the same first chair, the clearer the line tends to become.

The Experience Factor

In fact, experience is a great teacher for finding the line. Warren Schuh, Glenn Smith, and Robin Smith have all served as second chair leaders in multiple congregations. For each of them, the lessons learned in earlier positions were put to good use in subsequent second chair roles. Even as they faced bigger challenges, they achieved great success because of how they had grown in their previous roles. You do not have to leave for another second chair role to learn from experience; make a commitment to learn on the job and, in doing so, better define the line in your current position.

While Greg Hawkins was still relatively new in his role as executive pastor of Willow Creek Community Church, he always had special projects he was working on. He tended to do the research and then present several options without recommendation to his senior pastor, Bill Hybels. Over time, he realized that Bill wanted him to do more than just list alternatives; he was looking to Greg to make a recommendation. Not only did Greg need to make recommendations, he should make them with conviction. Greg learned to apply a "flinch test" to any presentation he was going to make. He began to assume that Bill was going to ask, "What would you do?" If Greg's reaction was to flinch as he made the recommendation, then he was not ready yet. By learning through these experiences, Greg became much more valuable as a second chair leader at Willow Creek.

Experience is an important teacher, but beware of relying too much on prior experience, particularly with other first chair leaders. How the line is defined with one first chair may not be applicable to someone else.

When Mike was a second chair lay leader in a prior church, the senior pastor asked for advice on the process for discerning a vision for the congregation. After all, this was an area in which Mike had extensive experience in business and as a church consultant. As Mike described his recommendations, he emphasized the importance of communication, specifically using sermons during the weekly worship services as a prime opportunity for communicating with the entire congregation. The pastor took offense at this; his sermon topics were a personal matter that he determined through prayer. He did not want anyone to suggest what he should preach on. When Mike came to West University several years later, he was reluctant to make any suggestions for sermon topics. His experience had taught him that to do so was clearly crossing the line beyond his role. When the subject of possible future sermon topics was raised during a staff retreat, Mike was quiet at first. He eventually explained his hesitation to comment, but our senior pastor made it clear that he would welcome input and would not see it as infringing on his ability to make the final decision on a series.

The Ego Factor

Another line-defining factor we do not like to talk about in ministry is ego. Your first chair's ego has considerable impact on your relationship and on how your role is defined. First chairs with fragile egos are usually uncomfortable with anyone who might be perceived as a stronger leader than themselves. Their actions, directly or indirectly, attempt to control their subordinates and keep them from taking a prominent leadership role. In a related vein, some first chairs have large egos that need constant stroking. They always need to be seen as the leader, which may leave little room for their second chairs to establish themselves. On the positive side are the first chair leaders who are secure in their own identity and in their role. They do not feel threatened by the second chair and know that their own effectiveness is enhanced if other leaders in the organization are allowed to thrive. Dena Harrison says, "If 'number one' has a healthy ego and is not threatened, 'number two' won't feel constrained." Think about your own first chair. What are his or her ego needs? Even if you think that they are out of line, they define your reality for this season of ministry.

The first chair is an important part of the ego factor, but the second chair's ego is equally significant. In what ways do your own ego needs enhance or detract from your relationship with your first chair? If your role is behind the scenes but you feel a need to be in a highly visible position, tensions are likely to escalate. If you want to have sole responsibility for a

realise what you can work on

particular ministry area and instead have supporting roles in many areas, you may experience frustration. Every time you try to define the line according to your ego needs, you run the risk of conflict. Recognizing and managing these needs helps improve your relationship with your first chair.

Warren Schuh found himself frustrated with the changes that were brought about by a new senior pastor. Most were minor, but they still required adjustment in his role. Once he stepped back and looked at the bigger picture, he realized that his reaction was not justified. Part of Dena Harrison's secret to success in three disparate second chair roles was her ability to push her ego demands to the side and focus on the Kingdom work that lay before her. Second chair leaders need to learn to read and manage the first chair's ego. They also need to accept that some of their needs may not be met until a later season. Doing this surely improves results and increases satisfaction in the second chair.

A Subtle Line

These stories illustrate an important aspect of the line for second chair leaders: it is subtle. This is another reason that job descriptions and following directions (from the first chair) are an inadequate way of defining the line. Even though Greg Hawkins was doing the special projects Bill Hybels asked him to do, there was a subtle but important difference between presenting well-researched findings and developing recommendations with conviction. The ways in which Dena Harrison demonstrated subordination in each second chair role varied because of the personalities and egos of her first chairs. She says, "Negotiating this paradox [subordinate-leader] is a highly nuanced skill. Difficulties arise when the skill of 'nuancing' is lacking."

There are many other subtleties. For example, Mike usually has strong opinions on any subject and is accustomed to speaking his mind anytime. He has had to learn when he can disagree with our senior pastor, and when he should be quiet. Differences of opinion are acceptable in staff meetings, but significant disagreements over future direction are best resolved one-on-one. Roger is responsible for budget preparation at West University, and as with most churches salaries are a large portion of our budget. One subtlety of his role is that he is free to develop next year's budget in all program areas, but our senior pastor wants to work directly with the personnel committee to develop the budget for salaries and benefits. This is not the kind of thing that can be written into a job description or explained in an interview. The subtleties are learned in real time through real experience.

The subtleties are important in any working relationship, but they are especially important between the first and second chairs. This is because so much of their effectiveness depends on trust and a common understanding of purpose. If you are not trusted and do not have a broad range of responsibility as a second chair leader, then you cease to be effective. If you misread the subtleties that define the lines for your role, then trust erodes.

A Moving Line

Just to make the challenge more difficult, the line is not static. Sometimes circumstances outside your control cause the line to move. It might shift inward toward you, giving you less freedom and authority in the organization. Or it might move outward, giving you a broader role. We are not primarily concerned about explicit movement of the line—those times when the first chair tells you your responsibilities are being changed. The real challenge is when the line moves but the change is not clearly articulated. These shifts can happen for any number of reasons.

For example, when one ministry in the church becomes a hot spot, the line tends to move. Several years ago, the children's ministry at West University was not one of our strengths. Because of our desire to reach young families, our senior pastor spent a considerable amount of his time focusing on this ministry. He wanted to know all that was happening, and he was involved in all the important decisions. Today, this same ministry receives much less of his attention, even though it is even more vital now than it was then. What has changed? We now have a strong leader in charge of the ministry (Barbara Chrisman), and she has developed a capable team to support her. The ministry is one of the strengths of the church. Furthermore, as Roger fully moved into his second chair role, he began to offer some oversight for this ministry. Clearly, the lines shifted, even though many of the changes were gradual and never formally announced.

You may feel the line is becoming more restrictive. Rather than having more freedom and autonomy, you seem to have less. You are being asked to get approval on more decisions and are being given more direction by your first chair. If this is happening, it may be that your first chair is losing confidence in you. This does not mean you have failed or that you should give up. You should, however, examine whether you have done anything to cause a loss of confidence or breach of trust. Are there performance problems in any of the areas for which you are responsible? Have you made a major decision that had unintended, negative consequences? Beyond this self-examination, you should also discuss the situation with your first chair. If you have the kind of healthy relationship we discussed in Chapter Three, this should be a positive conversation. It is possible that he is not even aware of how his behavior seems to be more controlling. Or he may have a specific issue that he has been hesitant to address. Either way, it is better to deal with any concerns openly and constructively.

It is also possible that restrictive movement of the line is due to external, uncontrollable circumstances. Tension or crisis in another part of the organization often causes a first chair leader to try to exert more control in all its parts. If a major change is pending, the first chair may be determined to prevent anything extraneous from rocking the boat. If members of the congregation are upset because of performance issues in a particular area, the senior pastor may become more insistent on a high level of performance in all other areas. If you are unaware of the root of the problem, you may not see the underlying reason your own line is being moved. What you experience is a seemingly arbitrary shifting of the line. You know that your once-autonomous decisions are now subject to review and modification.

Theresa Barnes (not her real name) experienced significant moving of the line during her tenure as associate pastor of a midsized mainline church. For three years, she had a healthy, growing relationship with the long-tenured senior pastor. He regularly asked for her advice and added to the scope of her responsibility. Then the church was named as the defendant in a large lawsuit. The senior pastor found much of his time occupied by preparations for this legal battle. As a result, the lines began to move and Theresa took on a more visible role in leading the congregation. Even though nothing changed officially, she was soon handling most of the day-to-day management, interaction with members, and committee administration. As the legal battle dragged out, the senior pastor became distracted and distant. After nearly three years, the suit was finally resolved, and the senior pastor was ready to resume his regular role. He seemed somehow to resent the way Theresa had filled the gap in his absence. The line began to move back the other way, to the point where she enjoyed even less autonomy and responsibility than before the problems began. Theresa left after two more years because she felt this was the best way to avoid crossing a line that had become too restrictive.

Where are the lines for your role? Do you have a clear understanding of them? Has the understanding been tested and verified by your experiences in this position and your relationship with your first chair? If you have never thought about the subtleties that yield the texture of a second chair's role, now is the time to do so. To be an effective second chair leader, you must be attuned to the constantly changing organizational currents that inevitably affect you and your role.

Crossing the Line

If you do not know exactly where the line is located, there is a good chance you will cross it. Even if you have a clear understanding of the line, you may still step over it sometime in your career. But be warned: crossing the line is a risky thing to do. Any time you cross it, your relationship with your first chair suffers and trust is eroded. As we have already discussed, a second chair leader cannot function effectively without a trust-based relationship at the top.

Crossing Accidentally

What happens when you cross the line accidentally? You start a new program without input from your senior pastor because you thought you had a green light. Or you move an administrative position from part-time to full-time because the funding was already in the budget. Your first chair may confront you over the decision. In this case, you have an opportunity to ask for clarification and apologize for overstepping your authority. If your relationship with the first chair is positive, the apology should be accepted as sincere and the incident soon forgotten. But you should not forget. It helped define the line for you, and if you do it again the second time will not be an innocent mistake.

Greg Hawkins is a successful and experienced second chair leader, but this did not save him from accidentally crossing the line. The church faced significant financial challenges after the September 11, 2001, terrorist attacks. After an intense period of considering all their options, the management team decided layoffs would be necessary. Greg helped design the process for prioritizing ministries and evaluating staff members, so the necessary cutbacks could be made in the most strategic and least damaging way.

Shortly after the decisions were made, Bill Hybels had to leave the country for a series of conferences. Greg felt it was his job to take the actions already agreed on, so he made the first of several painful layoffs of senior-level staff members. Unfortunately, he misunderstood a subtle line. He was the executive pastor, and the affected staff members reported to him. Greg's actions were consistent with his job description, and in other churches they would have been exactly what the senior pastor wanted him to do, but not in this case. Bill believed strongly that he needed to be present when the layoffs occurred. Some relational damage was done, but Greg's quick apology for an honest mistake allowed them to return to a firm footing.

In this story, it was crystal clear to the second chair that he had crossed the line. In other situations, the offense is not so evident. Your first chair may never tell you that you have crossed the line, but you may be aware that he or she is acting differently. Unfortunately, this is often the case. Some first chairs tend to avoid conflict. They may be the boss, but they would still rather not express their frustrations with a staff member. At other times, the first chair is too busy to confront the issue and decides to deal with it later. In the meantime, however, an element of unexplained stress creeps into the relationship.

Then there are the first chair leaders who live in constant tension because they feel uncomfortable or even threatened by the second chair. They are not happy with the official level of authority given to the subordinate. When the second chair leader hires an intern, the first chair is hesitant to say, "You're supposed to check with me before you hire someone." The hesitation comes from the knowledge that the hiring decision was completely within the second chair's defined authority but the first chair is still upset because she wanted to a have the final approval. Again, this frustration often manifests itself in strained relations between first and second chair.

Second chair leaders should notice the "relational trend lines" with their first chair. If the trend is in a negative direction, they should first examine their own actions and see if they might have done anything to cause offense. If they are genuinely unaware, then they should ask the first chair directly. Even if the first chair is unwilling or unable to articulate an answer, the second chair has tried to make the relationship right and indicated a desire to understand and stay within the lines.

In the best case, the second chair feels freedom to take risks, even those that are near the line. Of course, if you are trying new ideas, you are bound to have some failures. Bob Johnson's senior pastor, Jim Jackson, gave these directions to Bob: "We're all in the boat together, and I want you to take risks. It's OK to punch some holes in the boat; just try not to punch below the water line." Bob says that he spent his first year at Chapelwood trying to determine the exact location of the water line. He says, "I've punched a few holes below the water line in the process, but the boat hasn't sunk and I haven't been thrown out." If a second chair crosses a line accidentally, a strong relational foundation and the right motives are usually sufficient for the interpersonal and organizational damage to be repaired quickly.

Crossing Intentionally

The more troubling type of line crossing is intentional. This occurs when a second chair leader has a clear understanding of where the line is drawn and decides to cross it anyway. Put quite simply, this is insubordination. When you cross a significant line on purpose, you abandon the subordinate-leader paradox. You decide that it is more important to be right on an issue than in right relationship. Except in rare cases, crossing the line intentionally is unacceptable.

The distinction between disagreement and insubordination is an important one. Having a difference of opinion with your senior pastor is not crossing the line; telling others in the congregation about the disagreement is. Telling the executive director you believe he is making a mistake by not funding your proposal is not insubordination; going behind his back to get it funded is. Healthy relationships allow differing ideas. They have room for intense conflict because of these differences. But at the end of the disagreement, it is essential for the first and second chair to stand together and present a united front.

If you have the misfortune of working for a first chair who is a true autocrat, then you may find that any disagreement is seen as insubordination. In this case, you are being pushed to the other extreme of the subordinate-leader paradox and are prevented from truly leading. As we discuss in the final paradox, God may use your dreams and your call as a leader to move you out of this specific situation. Even in this most restrictive circumstance, however, taking action in direct opposition to your first chair is wrong; it undermines the Kingdom and ultimately undermines your career.

Mike has taught a variety of seminars based on his previous book, *Leading Congregational Change* (Herrington, Bonem, and Furr, 2000). They focus on building a strong, healthy future by understanding the dynamics of congregational transformation. Frequently during the breaks in these seminars, a second chair leader (or group of leaders) will approach Mike to talk about their church. They describe their excitement about the congregation's future potential and their role in leading change. Then, after an awkward pause, they often ask, "Can we do this if our senior pastor is not ready to make the needed changes?" Mike's answer is an unequivocal no. It will not work right; and it is not the right way to work. The former because change leadership requires the first chair to be the lead leader. The latter because the second chair leader must live with the tension of the subordinate-leader paradox and should not cross the line. The Bible has a clear word for this in Hebrews 13:17: "Obey your leaders and submit to their authority. . . . Obey them so that their work will be a joy, not a burden, for that would be of no advantage to you."

Two second chair leaders in a Houston area church did not understand this principle. Their congregation needed to become more contemporary and relevant to reach the surrounding community, but their senior pastor was reluctant. The younger second chairs decided they could not wait on their first chair, so they staged a leadership coup. They resigned their positions and started a new church a short distance away. They called each member of their former church to recruit people to join the new endeavor. Even if they sensed God calling them to do something new, and even if their former church needed a little shake-up, their tactics crossed the line. In the end, the former church was gutted, the senior pastor was heartbroken, the church plant was struggling, and they were left to deal with their insubordination.

Is it ever permissible to cross the line? We offer two rare cases in which to consider crossing the line, but even in these instances you should proceed with prayerful caution. If you have been seriously mistreated by your first chair, it may be appropriate to seek outside assistance. We are not talking about a simple conflict or hurt feelings; "serious mistreatment" is a pattern of harmful behavior that cannot be tolerated—verbal abuse, lack of integrity, or similar conduct. Even in this difficult situation, you should try to address the issue directly with the first chair. If it cannot be resolved, then seek guidance from an independent advisor, such as a judicatory leader. You may even solicit feedback from a key lay leader, but only if you can do so without the risk of spreading gossip or undermining the first chair.

The second case occurs if you are certain that the first chair is guilty of a serious moral or ethical failure. Perhaps he has admitted his wrong to you but told you not to tell anyone else. If you believe he has disqualified himself from leadership because of this action and is unwilling to resign, your role as a second chair leader requires that you take action. As in the first case, seek help from a denominational officer or lay leader.

Instances of either type should be rare. Losing an argument is not an excuse to seek outside help. Failure of a new program that was championed by the first chair is not the same as moral failure. In addition to being rare, both instances of line crossing are costly. In either case, even though you are doing the right thing, you should be prepared to lose your job. You may be terminated by the first chair for crossing the line. You may keep your job but find your relationship with the first chair has been strained to the point where you cannot function effectively. Even if the first chair leaves, you may also have to step aside to give the organization a fresh start.

Changing the Line

Maybe this entire chapter is too elementary for you. Suppose you already have a clear awareness of the lines defining your role and the risk of crossing them. Your issue is not definition; you are simply unhappy with the location of those lines. Your question is, "How can I redesign my role or my authority in a way that will lead to better results for the organization and be more fulfilling for me?" Said another way, "Can these lines be changed? If so, how?"

Many second chairs who want to move the line are seeking to expand the scope of their responsibility and authority. If this is the case, the first question to ask yourself is, "Am I excelling in my current responsibilities?" Just like the parable of the talents in Matthew 25, you should be faithful and productive with whatever you have been given. A first chair is not going to expand your duties if you underperform in your current role.

Sometimes the change is not one of expanding a role but shifting it, shedding some tasks and taking on others. There can be many reasons for doing so. You may be uniquely suited to a potential new task. Someone else may have a particular talent for one of your current assignments. You may feel burned out by the routine and are looking for a new challenge. Whatever the case, the first step is being faithful with the tasks you have been given. Once you have done that, you can begin to find a way to move the line rather than crossing it.

Moving the line ultimately requires interaction with the line setter: your first chair. But before you begin the conversation, examine your own motives. Why do you want to move the line? Mike spent a number of years as a business leader and business consultant, often encountering people who wanted to move the line. In the majority of cases, they had well-developed arguments for why the line should be moved, but they also had an ulterior motive. The direction of the move was always going to give them more—more power, a larger budget, more staff to supervise, greater visibility in the organization. If the line movement that you propose is for your glory rather than God's, turn around. Even if your motives are pure, ask yourself if the changes you propose could be *misconstrued by others* as self-promoting. You might suggest the right change but in the wrong way. If your tone suggests you are the hero riding to the church's rescue, you will lose influence even if you move the line. We deal with this further in Chapter Six.

Another part of your self-examination is to test the value to come from the change. The primary question your first chair will ask is, "How does this change benefit our ministry?" Whatever responsibilities you are proposing to add, can you do them well? If you add new tasks to your existing workload, what is sacrificed? If you are shifting some responsibilities, who will assume the duties you are dropping, and is this person qualified to do them? It is not enough to say, "I've been here for several years, so I deserve a bigger (or different) role."

Any time you want to change a line, trust and communication with your first chair are essential. Your first chair has to trust your motives, and you must trust the first chair to seek the best solution for you and the ministry. Communication is more than asking, "Can I make this change in my job description?" Communication needs to be an open dialogue in which various options are considered and the benefits honestly evaluated. Second chairs should be willing to consider solutions other than the ones they envision.

Soon after Geoff Surratt of Seacoast Church moved into a second chair role, he identified one line that should move. Several of the people who were now under Geoff's supervision had previously reported to the senior pastor, his brother Greg. Their behavior did not change with Geoff's promotion; they continued to consult with Greg on the important decisions in their ministry. Geoff could have gotten angry and accused the leaders of circumventing him, but he realized the bigger issue was the line defining first and second chair roles. There was nothing wrong with Greg's answers; the problem was that Greg was giving an answer. So long as he continued to be the answer man, these leaders would bypass Geoff. Geoff and Greg talked about the issue, and Greg agreed a change should be made. The shift in the line was subtle but significant. Whenever one of the staff members came to Greg, he would respond, "That sounds like a Geoff question." Even if Greg wanted to dig deeper, he would do so in a private conversation with Geoff.

If you are relatively new in a second chair role, it is best to assume that the line is more restrictive than you have been told. Why? Because it probably is. More important, this forces you to overcommunicate with your first chair. As the communication flows, you have a clearer understanding of the real location of the line, and the first chair has a better understanding of who you are and how you lead. If you are not sure whether you have the authority to make a decision, get his input on the specific decision. Then ask, "Is this the kind of decision I need to talk with you about, or should I just let you know once the decision is made?" Consider the situation from your first chair's perspective. If you make the decision without any communication, he may be glad to have someone who takes initiative. But he may also decide you are always going to push the line, and as a result he may be less willing to give you additional autonomy. Communication is a critical aspect of moving the line.

Moving the line may be easy in some organizations and difficult in others. Some first chairs are resistant to change. They do not want a second chair who is constantly looking for new challenges and always seeking to move the lines. For others, the issue is control or insecurity. Moving the line to give more autonomy or responsibility to second chair leaders feels too risky. In a situation like this, the second chair must remember the subordinate side of the paradox and practice patience. This does not mean giving up, but it does mean trusting the first chair's motives and judgment. It means explaining your perspective, listening to your first chair, and waiting to see if the changes are made over time. As we will see in the last paradox, God can use a time of prayerful waiting for great spiritual and professional development in your life.

Living with the Line

For as long as you are a second chair leader, the line is not going away. (In truth, first chair leaders have lines as well.) Your challenge is to learn to live with the line and manage it. As Greg Hawkins said, "I have to act like he [Bill Hybels] doesn't exist, and I have to act like he does exist, at the same time." If you pretend your first chair (and the lines he establishes) does not exist, then you will always be in trouble for crossing the line. If you dwell on the line and its seeming inequities, you will be unable to lead effectively.

The line is neither good nor bad. Some may see it as a hindrance, or even as something designed to trip them. Others may see it as a source of guidance and protection against being overloaded. In truth, it can be either. Boundary lines are simply the reality of any job, second chair or otherwise. For the second chair, they are just more complex and less clearly defined.

Living with the line does not equate with an attitude of frustration or resignation. Do not think of the line as a prison. Rather, it is a challenging balancing act. It requires the second chair leader to make the very best of the role. It requires the genius of the *and*—a second chair who is a loyal and dependable subordinate *and* who is a highly effective leader.

The best solution whenever the line seems too restrictive is to turn it over to God. Make the situation a matter of focused prayer, and while you do so continue to serve your leader and your organization with excellence. God may move the line, or He may move you to a new place of ministry. Or He might even change your perspective on the line. Our hope is that your leadership will rise to a new level as you learn to live—and thrive—with the line.

A WORD TO FIRST CHAIRS
ON THE SUBORDINATE-LEADER PARADOX

IF YOU ARE IN THE FIRST CHAIR in your church or organization, do you want your direct reports to be second chair *leaders*? The emphasis is on *leader* because the actions and attitudes of some first chairs work against our definition of a second chair leader. Enabling subordinates to lead is a theme that runs through each of these "Word to First Chairs" sections. If you want your second chairs to be leaders, you must be prepared to pay the price.

Now, your response may be, "What price? I'm the first chair, and I should make the rules." There may be truth in this, but allowing the high-potential individuals in your organization to lead requires an investment on your part. It costs some of your time to build relationships and interact with them. It requires you to release some of your power to them so they can make decisions and take action. It involves taking risks and allowing them to experiment, and at times fail.

We are convinced that the benefits far outweigh the costs. In fact, it is impossible for any entity to reach its full potential if everything depends on a single first chair. For your ministry to achieve all that God desires, it is essential to develop and release second chair leaders. Greg Hawkins of Willow Creek says, "I have to view myself as a leader to do my job. I'm not doing my job if I'm just an administrator." Not only does Greg have to view his role this way; his senior pastor, Bill Hybels, must have the same perspective. So in the context of the subordinate-leader paradox, how can this be done?

Reduce the Gap

Tom Billings, executive director of Union Baptist Association (UBA) in Houston, has occupied first and second chair roles in his career. His reflections from both sides of the fence offer helpful insight into the subordinate-leader paradox. Prior to his current first chair role, Tom was in a second chair position at UBA. At that time, the executive director, Jim Herrington, made a commitment to form a "director team," composed of Jim plus Tom and two other second chair leaders. They made a firm commitment that they would not make any major decisions without consensus from the entire team. Jim even tried to take it one step further by asking UBA's Personnel Committee to give each team member (including himself) the title of codirector. The committee affirmed Jim's intent, but they did not change anyone's title because they recognized that the association's outside constituents (local churches and local church pastors) needed to know "where the buck stops." Instead, the committee and the director team agreed that Jim's position of executive director could be structured so that it was "only one millimeter above the others." In contrast to a typical organizational hierarchy, the distance between first and second chairs, in terms of responsibility and authority, would be minimized.

Tom never really felt he was a subordinate in this structure. In his current first chair role, he continues to live by the one-millimeter philosophy. Dian Kidd, a second chair leader at UBA during Jim and Tom's tenures, describes this as "team by permission." She recognizes that Tom is the first chair, and the consensus-based approach to decision making requires his full commitment or it will not work. Does it work? UBA has operated by this philosophy for more than ten years and has experienced extraordinary results over that time. The association is widely recognized within Southern Baptist circles (and beyond) as one of the most effective and innovative judicatories in the country.

If you are a first chair leader, the decision is yours to make. Second chair leaders cannot shrink the gap between themselves and the top position. The decision rests in the hands of the first chair. Ask yourself these questions and take a minute to reflect: In your ministry, is the current gap, in terms of decision making and distribution of authority, more like one meter than one millimeter? How often do you give commands rather than seek consensus? Do you view your second chairs more as subordinates or ministry partners? Do you want to reduce the gap, and if so, what will it take to do so? Making decisions by consensus and permitting increased autonomy are the kinds of changes that reduce the gap and turn your subordinates into true second chair leaders.

Clarify Roles

"Reducing the gap" does not mean everyone has the same role or level of responsibility. As an organization grows and evolves, it is important for the first chair to articulate what is expected of all the senior leaders. In some cases, this begins in a discussion with the governing body (board, elders, deacons, session) to clearly define your own first chair role. Some boards take a "hands-off" approach, and others are highly involved. It is best to understand their expectations of you and their level of involvement as early as possible. They may also have specific ideas about the roles of the second chairs in the organization. As we saw in Chapter Four,

Glenn Smith's elder board and senior pastor were not on the same page when they promoted him into a second chair position.

In many cases, the governing body is not highly involved in defining the roles for second chair leaders. They may authorize the position, review the general job description, and approve the candidate. But it is typically left to the first and second chairs to work out the nuances of defining the line. As the lead leader, you should be aware that poorly defined lines can sap the energy from your ministry. If second chairs are unclear about their responsibility and authority, they are unable to lead effectively. We recognize that the lines can never be fully defined, but we encourage you to regularly discuss these important boundaries with the second chairs in your organization.

Build Trust

In Chapter Three, we described the importance of trust in the relationship between second chairs and their senior leaders. We encouraged second chair leaders to be "trust builders" in these relationships. First chairs must realize that building trust is a two-way street. How readily do you trust your second chairs? When they make a mistake, does it permanently affect your perception of their ability? If they disagree with you, do you interpret this as disloyalty? This does not mean all second chairs are loyal and trustworthy, or that they should not be corrected. It does mean your second chair leaders deserve the benefit of the doubt. As a first chair leader, you should be looking for reasons to trust and have confidence in those who work for you. Kouzes and Posner say it this way: "Trusting leaders give people the freedom to innovate and take risks. They nurture openness, involvement, personal satisfaction, and high levels of commitment to excellence. . . . Because they're more trusting of their groups, they're also willing to let others exercise influence over group decisions. It's a reciprocal process. By demonstrating an openness to influence, leaders contribute to building the trust that enables their constituents to be more open to the leader's influence. Trust begets trust" (2004, p. 28).

Some first chairs are afraid to trust. They may have been burned by trusting too much, or trusting the wrong person in the past. Their attitude is, "The risk and potential cost are too high for me to fully trust my subordinates." Our response is that the opportunity cost of not trusting is too high for you *not* to take the risk. If trust is not extended, second chairs cannot lead and the organization cannot reach its full potential.

If trusting others is difficult for you, examine why. Is some incident from a previous ministry setting preventing you from releasing your team today? Is there an outside coach or counselor who can help you understand the reasons? Are there small steps of trust you can take experimentally? This might be to disclose one specific area of insecurity. Or it might be to give your second chair total freedom on a project. Becoming a more trusting leader is not an overnight process; it happens one small step at a time.

Develop Relationships

Trust is just one important facet of the relationship between leaders. How would you rate the overall quality of your relationship with your second chairs? In this book we encourage second chairs to make their relationship with the first chair a top priority. Are you willing to give the time to let this relationship develop? Glenn Smith says, "Senior leaders should not spend personal capital on many things, because they need a big reservoir of personal capital. But the second chair is one thing they need to spend personal capital on."

This does not necessarily mean that you and they are best friends or spend lots of time together socially. But first chairs need to know what makes their second chairs tick. You should understand their strengths and weaknesses, their joys and hurts, the activities that drain energy from them, and the things about which they are passionate. You must know enough about their lives to show concern when they are experiencing difficulty, and to celebrate their victories. Frankly, they have to know the same things about you. Part of building a stronger relationship with your second chair is not giving the impression of an impassive leader who is always in control. Some leaders think that respect is earned by never admitting to a mistake, or fear, or uncertainty. In reality, a deeper level of respect is possible whenever relationships are honest and transparent. For the first chair, this means letting your second chairs see behind the mask to know what is happening on the inside. This can only be done in the context of a healthy, trusting relationship.

Model Your Faith

If you really want to see your second chairs reach their full potential as subordinates and leaders, look at how you are living out your faith. If those who follow you cannot see ample evidence of spiritual depth, if your walk does not match your talk, if you are not putting the Kingdom first in your life, then those who follow you will never achieve their full potential. Why? Because people in general, and leaders in particular, want to have deep respect for the leaders they follow. Without this respect, they cannot serve gladly and loyally. They cannot make the kind of commitment that allows them to excel.

We both have had times of conflict with our senior pastor, but we never doubt his heart for God and the depth of his commitment to seek and serve the Lord. The importance of this cannot be overstated. Anytime disagreement arises, we look to how he models his faith, and we cannot question his motives. We may disagree on a decision or a tactic, but we know that our core values are in alignment and that our ultimate desires for the ministry we share are the same. Disagreement between leaders is inevitable. It is the deeper, common faith and vision that sustain the relationship through periods of tension. In your first chair role, we hope your subordinates can say the same of you that we say of our senior pastor.

This principle was demonstrated in a pivotal moment at Union Baptist Association. The director team (which we have already described here) was still a relatively new concept when they had an all-day staff meeting to work on a major decision. The four team members were exhausted at the end of the day, but they also felt good about reaching a clear consensus on the issue. That evening, Jim Herrington wanted the rest of the staff to know the decision, so he left a group voicemail message to explain the meeting's outcome. When Dian Kidd, one of the director team members, heard the message the next morning, she was furious. The message was contrary to her understanding of the decision. Before she replied to the message or confronted Jim in some other way, she reflected further. She vividly recalls what went through her mind: "Do I really think that Jim is trying to undermine the whole team and the direction of UBA? Do I trust Jim?" Dian knew Jim's heart for God and his commitment to the director team and the organization. He had proven it many times as he lived out his faith and exemplified the vision of UBA. Rather than an angry, insubordinate response, the incident led to a clarifying of the miscommunication. More important, it brought Dian to a much deeper level of trust for her first chair leader. This result was possible only because of the consistency of Jim's words and his actions over many months prior to the event. Had he not repeatedly shown how he put his faith into practice, Dian would not have reached the same conclusion. Authentic faith is a first chair's greatest leadership asset.

Do you want true second chair leaders in your organization? Encourage them to be leaders. Clarify your role and theirs. Give them the freedom to lead, to take initiative, and to make some mistakes. Give them the benefit of the doubt whenever possible, and be the first in line to show trust in them. Invest in them with your time, personal interest, and encouragement.

Be a leader whose faith is evident to all and who models a deep commitment to Christ. As the Bible teaches, "Remember your leaders, who spoke the word of God to you. Consider the outcome of their way of life and imitate their faith" (Hebrews 13:7). Even though this verse is addressed to those in a subordinate role, it is an important challenge for you in the first chair to be the model your second chairs imitate.

DEEP-WIDE

SECOND CHAIR LEADERS live in the deep-wide paradox every day. They have no choice. Their role requires them to see the big picture and make decisions that affect the entire organization. It frequently requires them to delve into the details to solve a problem in some part of the organization, or to launch a new ministry. They move from a strategic planning meeting to analysis of why one department is over budget, from a discussion about the church's spiritual maturity to recruiting additional small-group leaders. If a first chair is not well versed in the details, it is excused because he or she is the "visionary leader," a big-picture person. But if a second chair misses either end of the deep-wide continuum, the person's performance might be considered "in need of improvement." Greg Hawkins says quite simply, "It's all about being deep and wide."

Joseph modeled deep-and-wide behavior when he was called upon to interpret Pharaoh's dreams (Genesis 41:14–32). We should be clear: Joseph's accurate interpretation of the dreams was a God-given revelation. But his insight into the far-reaching implications of the dreams and the practical solutions that he began to devise are a classic second chair response:

> Seven years of great abundance are coming throughout
> the land of Egypt, but seven years of famine will follow

them. Then all the abundance in Egypt will be forgotten, and the famine will ravage the land. . . . And now let Pharaoh look for a discerning and wise man and put him in charge of the land of Egypt. Let Pharaoh appoint commissioners over the land to take a fifth of the harvest of Egypt during the seven years of abundance. They should collect all the food of these good years that are coming and store up the grain under the authority of Pharaoh, to be kept in the cities for food. This food should be held in reserve for the country, to be used during the seven years of famine that will come upon Egypt, so that the country may not be ruined by the famine [Genesis 41:29–30, 33–36].

Joseph's recommendation allowed Egypt and Pharaoh to survive the famine and strengthen their political power for years to come. He saw how a famine would affect the country and its leader. He must have known the potential severity of the threat—starvation, political unrest, rebellion, and risk of attack by an adversary. Once his interpretation of the vision stopped, his deep-and-wide plan to rescue Egypt began. Because God had given him significant administrative gifts, Joseph saw how to take advantage of the coming seven years of abundance. He realized that the pending disaster could be averted with a well-run program of grain collection.

How do you collect 20 percent of the harvest from an entire nation? Joseph knew that the size of the famine relief task was larger than what any one person could accomplish. From the outset, his plan included others. He knew the depth of the problem and the width of its reach, so he devised a plan and a team that matched the scope of the challenge. Second chair leaders are not looking to be solo performers; they want and need the support of a team.

Seven years of famine sounds like a recipe for disaster. Even with the advance warning of Pharaoh's dream, most of us would simply hope to hang on and survive the lean years. But in these adverse circumstances, Joseph saw opportunity. Not only did he save the nation from starvation; he was able to acquire great wealth for Pharaoh: "Joseph collected all the money that was to be found in Egypt and Canaan in payment for the grain they were buying, and he brought it to Pharaoh's palace" (Genesis 47:14). Once their money was gone, the Bible tells us that Joseph then took their cattle in exchange for food, and ultimately their land and their freedom. In the midst of this great famine, Joseph clearly had Pharaoh's interest at heart. At the height of the famine, Joseph was able to successfully obtain the land of the Egyptian people for Pharaoh. His width allowed him to see the implications of the famine throughout the whole land, and his depth enabled him to turn this into a tremendous opportunity for Pharaoh. When his first chair then succeeded, Joseph experienced his greatest personal success and blessing as well.

Like Joseph, you can also experience God's blessings if you are deep and wide in the second chair. As you see the complete picture of the needs in your congregation or organization, you have opportunities to turn potential problems into positive solutions. You may have a direct hand in designing and implementing a new strategy that bears much fruit. You may diagnose and resolve an obstacle that has kept the ministry from rising to the next level. You may see opportunities that everyone else has overlooked. As you master the deep-wide paradox, your fulfillment and value as a second chair leader will reach a new height.

5

A MATTER OF PERSPECTIVE

[handwritten margin note: think systems theory]

CAN SOMEONE IN THE SECOND CHAIR really add value *throughout* the organization? After all, the second chair seems so restrictive at times. Is the ability to have such broad influence limited to those who have an official title that conveys organizationwide authority and responsibility? The truth is that adding value throughout the organization is not a function of position; it is a matter of perspective.

Mat Yelvington, our minister to students, has a passion for the teens in our congregation and for developing the best possible ministry for them. He has read all the best material on building a vibrant youth ministry. He pours himself into the kids. He is building a team of other leaders who share his heart and who understand the needs of this ministry. He has a growing, effective ministry that is a vital part of our congregation. But when Mat first joined our staff, his ideas and suggestions on churchwide issues often seemed to fall on deaf ears. It was not because he was the youngest or least-tenured person in the room, and it was not that his ideas lacked merit. The real reason was that Mat often failed to see how his suggestions might cause conflict or be impractical to implement. As he gained a broader perspective, his influence also increased, and we now frequently see him adding value throughout the organization.

Mat is not unique; we have all known and worked with people like him. Most of us can personally identify with Mat, in past or current roles. Churches are full of administrators who see everything through a financial lens, children's ministers who see everything through a kid's eyes, musicians who hear everything through a set of headphones, and teachers who think they own their class and classroom. As you move down the organization chart from the first chair, you find positions with ever more narrowly defined responsibilities. But effectiveness as a second chair leader requires that you see the big picture, even as you are continuing to serve with excellence in your functional role. This is the essence of the deep-wide paradox.

Second Chair or Second Tier?

Some second chair leaders primarily see the big picture. They spend their time thinking about the future and the possibility of what the congregation can become. They can paint an exciting picture of a church that reaches new people for Christ or has a dramatic impact on its community. They struggle, however, to understand the details and develop a plan of action. At worst, these individuals lose their leadership influence because they are labeled unproductive dreamers, people with great ideas but with no ability to follow through.

At the other end of the continuum are the leaders who have deep knowledge of their specific area of responsibility. They know every person in their ministry. They have in-depth plans for how every program in their realm should operate. You never worry about something falling through the cracks where they are involved. But they are sometimes criticized as hyperfocused and only interested in their area. They may be accused of being overprotective of their turf. They often fail to see how their actions and the activities in their ministry affect other parts of the congregation.

How did you get to your current position? How have you been successful in the past? Chances are that you excelled in one side of this paradox or the other. Perhaps you received kudos for being a great out-of-the-box thinker. Or you are the one people turn to when they want flawless implementation of a new program idea. Whichever is the case, you have probably developed a bias to continue doing what worked for you historically. The challenge is to recognize that this bias can be a handicap if you want to become a more effective second chair leader. If you want to be a deep-and-wide leader, you have to begin by developing an ability to see your organization from both deep and wide perspectives.

We have already stated that being a second chair leader is not a matter of position, but of influence. Think about people you have known who were in important roles, reporting directly to the first chair leader, but who did not fit our definition of a second chair leader. Whether their title was executive pastor, vice president, associate pastor, senior warden, or anything else that indicated significant positional authority, they did not consistently *add value throughout the organization*. It was not a question of whether people throughout the organization knew them, or whether they were involved in organizationwide activities, but whether or not you could see their impact on many parts of the organization. Was their advice sought out? When they spoke on a major issue, were their comments heard? If the answers to these questions are negative, then these are individuals we consider to be "second-tier," but not second chair leaders.

We have also seen the reverse scenario played out: a person whose official role seemed quite narrow but who had a large, positive impact on many other areas in the life of the organization. We are not talking about the squeaky wheel, the person who is heard simply by complaining loudly. We are talking about the lower-level staff member or lay leader who has limited positional authority but whose influence is felt because of the way he or she uses God-given wisdom and ability. In a recent strategic planning meeting at our church, one of our newer members brought clarity to a contentious point we had been struggling with for several weeks. His ability to see the bigger picture, connect with others, and communicate a valuable perspective made a major difference in our plans. Even though his only formal authority is that of Bible study teacher, his influence is much broader because of his ability to step outside his role and relate well with a variety of leaders in the church.

The View from Inside a Silo

Have you ever been in a meeting where someone released resources from his area so they could be used elsewhere? Isn't it a breath of fresh air when you encounter people who do not always defend their territory?

Many of us work and worship in organizations that are a collection of loosely connected "silos." An organization of this kind defines specific, functional responsibilities and assigns them to various second-tier leaders. Each person is supposed to carefully and completely execute his or her responsibilities within this organizational subunit and not worry about the rest of the organization. For example, one person in a denominational entity focuses on church planting, another on training and caring for clergy, a third on congregational revitalization. These seem to be separate, well-defined assignments. In theory, the person making the assignments (the first chair leader) is keeping an eye on the big picture.

The problem: no single individual, first chair or otherwise, can possibly integrate all the information required to maintain an accurate view of the entire organization. Furthermore, assignments are never neatly divided into such distinct responsibilities. If the programs for clergy training are not integrated with the church planting and congregational revitalization efforts, the denomination will experience redundancy or send confusing messages to its constituents. A person inside a silo finds it impossible to see anything more than the limited world in which he or she operates. We need more people—second chair leaders—to rise above their silos and help see and shape the organizationwide perspective.

Every organization has a certain amount of institutional inertia, which tends to be perpetuated by silos, as Gary Ferbet discovered. Memorial Drive Presbyterian, where Gary is executive pastor, has a rich heritage of giving generously to a variety of outreach ministries and mission agencies. In fact, half of the church's budget supports these outreach organizations. As the church was developing a new vision statement, the senior pastor wrote a white paper stating that evangelism, discipleship, and community impact should be their top priorities. He further explained that they should not be seen as three new programs; rather, they were to be integrated across all ministry areas.

Along with the church's new director of global missions, Gary advocated applying this principle in the church's funding decisions for external ministries. This was an above-the-silo approach, but they encountered quite a strong silo. Some currently funded mission agencies did not meet the criteria of doing all three priorities, so Gary and his colleague proposed a gradual phase out of funding. A vocal lay leader opposed this move, explaining, "That's not how we do it." The issue was resolved after some intense disagreement, but not before Gary learned about the resilience of silos.

Across the heartland of America, grain silos are a common sight. On the flat prairies, they are conspicuous. In business, the term is used to describe companies that fail to achieve cross-functional collaboration; this analogy can be applied to many churches and religious organizations today. Silos have well-defined functions; they store grain and dispense it at the appropriate time. An organizational silo also tends to have a specific description of its purpose and boundaries. A grain silo is made with hard, impenetrable walls that are designed to not let anything in or out. Likewise, have you ever had the unfortunate experience of making a suggestion to a territorial colleague on the staff? Looking from the outside, it is impossible to tell whether the silo is full or not. Have you ever wondered what really happens in a closed-door committee meeting, or why a particular ministry does not get more done? Silos also stand alone. They may be found in small groups, but there is no further connection to the next group of silos down the road. How much true connection exists between departments in your organization?

We are not saying that everyone in the church should be a generalist, or that the specific activities in each ministry area are unimportant. Quite the opposite; effective second chair leaders must first be responsible for their functional areas. But to be successful, they must move far beyond and above the silo mentality. This begins with breaking down the protective walls surrounding their own ministry area, by disclosing plans and activities, being honest about resource requirements, asking for input and feedback. As influence and relationships are built, these second chairs also have the opportunity to peer into other organizational silos and begin to complement the first chair's role of orchestrating the overall direction of the enterprise. It is this organizationwide perspective that is critical for any second chair leader. You cannot be an effective second chair leader, and your ministry will not excel, if you spend all your time trapped inside your silo.

What Do You See?

The familiar story of the blind men describing an elephant is an appropriate illustration of the struggles of many second chair leaders to be wide. Each blind man was touching a part of the elephant; the one touching its legs described an animal like a tree, the one touching the trunk described an oversized snake, and the one touching the ears described a birdlike creature. Each had only a part of the picture.

In Mike's consulting work, he meets with multiple leaders from the same congregation. There are times when he wonders if the people he has met are all part of the same church body. One leader describes a splintered and conflicted congregation, and another paints a picture of relational harmony. One talks about smooth and effective decision making, and someone else insists that the church is paralyzed by tradition. They are usually all correct to a point, but the real truth is a combination of their assessments. To lead effectively in the second chair, you must learn to see and understand the big picture—the entire elephant.

The parable of the blind men and the elephant, however, is misleading. Your reaction may be, "I'm not blind; my eyes are wide open. I have a good perspective on the whole church." Some people even become defensive when we imply that their perspective of their congregation is incomplete or distorted. You may not be blind, but everyone has blind spots or biases in looking at his or her organization. Perhaps a better analogy is to think about how individuals with good eyesight would describe the elephant. If you spend a day interviewing visitors to the zoo, you will hear many descriptions of the elephant. One person remarks on the size of the animal. Another laughs about its bathing rituals. Someone else talks about how slowly it moves, while another is surprised at how fast it moves given its size. Still another might be surprised at the long, stiff hair on the elephant's body. It is not a matter of one person having the right answer; they are all correct in their observations. But each person's observation is also incomplete, because he or she spends a limited amount of time watching the elephant. One's attention gravitates toward something specific, whether from individual interest or because of what the elephant happens to be doing at that moment.

Ask the zookeeper to talk about the elephant, however, and you get a much different story. The zookeeper might tell you that this particular elephant is actually a bit on the small side, compared to other zoo elephants. She might talk about how the elephant has just been ill and is a little sluggish today. She might talk about the several kinds of hair elephants have on various parts of their bodies.

Thriving in the deep-wide paradox begins with developing a perspective on your congregation that is as complete as possible. Those with limited perspectives are not bad people; nor are their intentions for the organization bad. We assume that they truly want the best for their church. But who is to define what "the best" is? Just like zoo visitors, we often spend very little time thinking about the overall picture, and as a result our perspective is limited and skewed by our particular biases.

Kim Miller, of Ginghamsburg Church, remembers learning this lesson. As she moved from being an "unpaid servant" into a formal role on the senior management team, the drama, music, and other multimedia aspects of the worship experience continued to be her primary focus. Then in the summer of 1999, Ginghamsburg went through a painful season. The leaders realized the church was strong in worship but weak in other areas. In Kim's words, "You can't grow a church through worship alone. If you try to do this, the people won't grow." This realization led to significant changes in Ginghamsburg's ministry approach. It also forced Kim to see and think more broadly. Her primary responsibility did not change, but she did gain a much better perspective on the overall health of the congregation.

Even as we try to see the bigger picture, we tend to see through a particular lens. If you ask various leaders in our church to describe its strengths, some will talk about its emphasis on teaching the Bible and others about children's ministry. Some will point to the music program and others talk about the friendliness and warmth of the congregation. All of these answers are accurate, and none of them are contradictory or mutually exclusive. They simply reflect the lenses through which the speaker sees.

Why is this so important for a second chair? Because second chairs are influencing decisions and priorities that affect the entire congregation. This question of perspective becomes more interesting if you ask what should be done to strengthen the congregation. Again, you will get differing answers, but if the available resources are limited, trade-offs will have to be made.

When this occurs, the importance of obtaining a clear perspective and overcoming your biases becomes much more obvious.

People fail to grasp the larger organizational perspective for any number of reasons. Some are simply not interested. They are satisfied with their position and responsibilities and are content to be told how they can fit into the broader strategy. These individuals are not second chair leaders as we have defined it. Others may be interested but lack the time. Some positions require so much time spent looking at the trees that the individual really cannot see the forest. Others lack the opportunity; they may be interested but are not part of the meetings and discussions that would help them take the broader view. Those who excel in the second chair, however, find ways to overcome these barriers of time and opportunity.

Learning to See Deeper and Wider

How can you develop a deep-and-wide perspective? The most important concept for learning to see deep and wide, for developing second chair insights into your congregation, is *systems thinking.* According to Peter Senge, a renowned expert on the subject, "Systems thinking is a discipline for seeing wholes. It is a framework for seeing interrelationships rather than things, for seeing patterns of change rather than static 'snapshots'. . . . Today, systems thinking is needed more than ever because we are becoming overwhelmed by complexity" (1990, pp. 68–69). Systems thinking helps you understand that a change in one aspect of the congregation ripples through the rest of the body. It is not possible to make one isolated adjustment and maintain the status quo everywhere else. In *Leading Congregational Change,* we used the phrase "every change changes everything" to help describe these dynamics (Herrington, Bonem, and Furr, 2000, p. 153).

For example, when a new children's minister is hired, the boost to this ministry brings more young families into the church. This requires the addition of new adult Bible study classes (and teachers). It also subjects the facilities to the critical eyes of parents who want only the best for their young children. The ripple effect can be far-reaching. Or consider what happens when a church becomes more evangelistic and begins to reach unchurched people in its community. A "Christianity 101" course might be needed because the new believers are not comfortable with the foundational level of Bible knowledge that is presumed in the church's regular Bible study groups. The pastor might have to change the sermon content or style to communicate more effectively to this audience. The Christian education director might spend much more time answering questions about how to live a faith-filled life. As these shifts occur, some of the long-time members might become upset because "our needs are not being met."

An ability to think systemically is a key difference between second chair leaders and those in the second tier. Some people are naturally gifted at seeing and understanding the dynamics of complex organizational systems. But even if this is not your innate ability, you can learn to do it better. Where should you start? Begin by spending time with the first chair leader in your organization—the senior pastor, executive director, bishop, president. Admittedly, not all first chairs are gifted at systems thinking and seeing the big picture, but most who fill the role successfully have learned to think this way. Try to see the organization through their eyes. Let them explain their reasoning for a particular decision. Learn how they see your ministry in the context of the larger organization. This helps you see the big picture; it also strengthens your relationship with the first chair.

Serving in a pastoral role on a church staff has been a learning process for Mike. Even though he learned much about leadership in the business world, he discovered he was unprepared for some of the subtle differences in church leadership. During his first two years at West University, he would often meet one-on-one with our senior pastor to gain insight on a particular issue. He would ask for counsel or for the rationale behind a decision, even if it did not relate to his specific ministry area. This process helps Mike have a wider and more complete perspective.

Learning to ask questions is a valuable practice that should extend beyond your first chair to others as well. Too many people, especially those who have had ministry or leadership training, grow accustomed to *telling* rather than *asking*. Their self-image is based on being the person with the answers. They see asking questions as a sign of weakness or incompetence.

Asking questions is the best way to gain a more complete perspective on your congregation. If you always have the answers, you will never grow in your knowledge and understanding. What should you ask? Lots of *why* questions. Why did our attendance increase so much this year? Why do you think this person reacted so strongly to my proposal? Why do so few of the participants in our preschool program attend our worship services? Why do our people not seem to invite their friends to church with them? Why have we not seen our annual stewardship campaign improve from year to year?

Also ask lots of *what-if* questions. As you do, continue to press for second- and third-order implications. What will happen if we add a second worship service? The immediate answer to this might be negative: "It will split the congregation, and we will have two struggling services in-

though we can't guarantee cause–effect

stead of one vibrant one." Do not be satisfied with this initial answer. What if we use this as an opportunity to recruit and develop a new group of leaders? Will that change the negative perception? What if the second service is designed for a group that is on the margin of our congregation, or one we are struggling to reach? Getting beyond the superficial answers is a great benefit of this kind of questioning. Combining the *why* and *what-if* questions can produce a rich understanding of organizational dynamics.

When West University Baptist was first thinking about adding a contemporary worship service, we did not ask enough *what-if* questions. We surveyed the congregation to assess the number who were interested in this option, and we expected 35–40 percent would switch to the new service. We believed this would give us a large enough core to make the new service viable, and leave enough behind to maintain strength in the traditional service. What *what-if* questions might we have asked? What if more people than expected make this switch? What if an important group, such as members of the choir, do not follow our plan? What if parents and their kids, or husbands and wives, disagree on the choice of service? It turned out that all of these were problems for us. Our first experiment with a contemporary service did not work as we had hoped. Perhaps a better analysis of the second-order effects would have made a difference.

The point of asking questions is that they help you gain a broader perspective. The questions can be directed to anyone, not just the first chair or a colleague on staff. As you ask questions, be diligent in looking for the hidden connections between parts of the congregation. Be hesitant to accept the first, simple answer to any question you ask. A guiding principle of systems thinking is "solving the problem can make things worse." That is to say, the real problem is often not addressed with a quick-fix solution. If one department is consistently over budget, the quick answer may be to increase its budget or reprimand the department head. The deeper solution requires investigating the cause of the overrun and possibly reprioritizing programs within the department, or collaborating with another ministry area.

Questions are a two-way street. Being on the receiving end of questions is also a valuable practice for second chairs who want to see deep and wide. The problem is many of us are too defensive or protective of our areas. We allow the first chair to ask questions about our programs and activities because he or she is the boss and some scrutiny is expected. But how often do you ask a fellow staff member or a key lay leader to review an idea and offer constructive feedback? Admittedly, negative feedback may not be helpful and can be difficult to hear. It may be embarrassing to be asked questions about a ministry proposal and not know the answer.

The question "Have you thought about . . . ?" carries the implication that you have not anticipated something important. As a result, many second chair leaders seek input only when the first chair requires them to do so, or when they are working on a cross-organizational initiative.

Our advice is simple: if what you are doing is important, and if you want to grow as a second chair leader, then swallow your pride and ask for feedback. Do so even if you are sure you have the best answer, even if you do not think you have time, even if you hate criticism. The immediate benefit is important enough: you can achieve better results. The long-term benefit is even greater: you can grow in your ability to understand the dynamics of the congregational systems.

It is impossible to be an effective second chair leader if you cannot see the big picture. Make a commitment to expand your perspective through conversations with your first chair, asking questions of all the key leaders in the organization, and seeking feedback on the work you are doing. Make this a practice, and you will find you are able to see the congregation and all of its dynamics in a different light.

Not Just the Big Picture

We have all known the stereotypical visionary leader with lots of great ideas that lack practicality and are never implemented. That is not what we are talking about when we describe a second chair leader who excels at being deep and wide, who has a knack for systems thinking. Systems thinking requires seeing the forest *and* the trees.

Attention to the details begins with seeing the trees in your own area of responsibility. Maybe this goes without saying, but we have known more than a few second chair leaders who have big dreams and little follow-through. If you are responsible for the church's mission efforts, be sure that they are done with excellence. Identify new mission opportunities, recommend which ones should be pursued, create and implement plans for the recommendations that are approved, and monitor their results. If you lead the senior adult ministry, get to know the stories and joys and hurts of these men and women. Be available in their times of crisis. Help them feel valued and stay involved in the life of the congregation. Organize activities and ministries that appeal to them.

As a second chair leader, however, your attention to detail must extend beyond your specific assignments. Once you have a clear understanding of the overall vision for the congregation and you practice systems thinking, you will begin to see gaps that are not being addressed. They usually

talk — about how to ask for feedback

relate to something new or different that can strengthen the organization but that do not fall neatly into a defined ministry area. For example, suppose you want to survey recent visitors to get feedback on their experience; whose responsibility is this? Who will launch a new leadership development process that identifies and mentors high-potential individuals and places them in roles where they can learn and be tested as congregational leaders? In reality, just as many possibilities for organizational improvement fall in the gaps as fit into well-defined program areas. Many ministry leaders simply do not see these opportunities. They are focused on their own area. But effective second chair leadership recognizes and prioritizes these options.

A second chair perspective includes the larger organizational picture, the details assigned to your ministry areas, and the opportunities in the gaps. It also includes the needs that are in the areas for which other people are responsible. This aspect of deep-wide is more sensitive. After all, who am I to tell a colleague or another leader how to improve his or her ministry? We examine the relational aspects of this in the next chapter. For now, consider how much you know about the work that is being done in other ministries or departments in your congregation or organization. In a silo-based model, only the first chair leader has this knowledge. Yet the first chair in a large organization cannot possibly understand all the areas or see all the connections and issues.

The most valuable second chair leaders develop a deep-and-wide perspective that extends throughout the organization. They become knowledgeable of the key aspects of all ministry areas. They do so without being unduly intrusive and without damaging relationships with their peers. They seek this knowledge to improve the organization's overall effectiveness. In fact, their greatest contribution is in seeing the connections between silos and finding solutions that cross organizational boundaries.

What Is My Job?

For most second chair leaders, seeing the big picture and looking into the details throughout the organization raises an important question: What is my job description? In Chapter Four, we discussed how written job descriptions rarely convey the true responsibilities for second chair leaders. The wide part of the paradox almost sounds as if their role duplicates that of the first chair, right? Yes and no. Yes, because we are saying that a second chair leader needs to think like a first chair by taking an organizationwide perspective and making decisions on the basis of this comprehensive view.

But no, because second chairs must never forget that their position is subordinate. They must have a clear understanding of role and authority so as not to cross the line.

A typical job description, particularly for church staff members, has a list of specific responsibilities and ends with a final point saying ". . . and other duties as assigned by the senior pastor." This is a catch-all phrase recognizing that the individual might be called on to do any number of activities. The perfect job description for second chair leaders should be written something like this:

o Always support the first chair leader. Support him or her through your loyalty, your encouragement, and by taking on specific duties as they are assigned. Gain a clear understanding of the authority that he or she is giving you, and always keep him or her informed of any significant undertakings or issues.

o Always think of the needs of the congregation (or organization) ahead of any specific tasks. Identify and act upon ideas that enable the organization to operate more effectively and, in doing so, to better fulfill its vision. These ideas are likely to cut across organizational boundaries.

The specific responsibilities for the position should be listed *after* these two points. The true second chair leader must think organization first, specific ministry assignment second. The specific ministry, however, has to be a close second. As we have emphasized, being deep *and* wide is a defining characteristic of the effective second chair leader.

Kim Miller says, "Most people don't make it onto a senior management team because their wiring does not allow them to see the wide picture." If you do not have a wide-angle lens, then work to develop one. Seeing and acting on the larger perspective is critical, but it is also risky. Any time second chair leaders start acting from this organizationwide perspective, they open themselves up to criticism from others who think they are grabbing for power. Dealing with these relational risks and capitalizing on relational opportunities is the focus of the next chapter.

6

BUILDING THE TEAM . . .
ONE RELATIONSHIP AT A TIME

FOR GREG HAWKINS, the path to becoming the executive pastor at Willow Creek was through relationships. We have already discussed the importance of the relationship between a second chair and the senior pastor, and that was an important ingredient in Greg's case. In January 1996, after facilitating Willow Creek's first strategic planning process, Greg was asked to join the senior management team and lead implementation of the plan. In this untitled role, he was given complete access to the organization and a large responsibility, but no one reported directly to him. It was truly a position with all authority and no authority.

When Greg was given the title of executive pastor in mid-1997, he became the only direct report to Bill Hybels; the rest of the staff reported to Greg. Even though this sounds like a major shift, it was a smooth, almost unnoticed transition. Why? Implementation of the strategic plan required Greg to interact and build relationships all across the organization. By the time the position was formalized, everyone already saw Greg as a leader among peers. Greg says, "I think that Bill [Hybels] was waiting for the others to reach the point where they wanted this change to happen."

Too many second chair leaders think they have to wait for formal authority—as indicated by lines and boxes on an organization chart—before they can truly have an impact on their organization. This story illustrates again that leadership is influence. In fact, a staff member who cannot lead through influence should not be given additional authority. The second chair who waits to be given the reins of control is unlikely to be an effective leader if or when that authority is extended.

Influence with peers is tricky. The moment you try to get involved in a situation outside your specific area of responsibility, you risk conflict ("Stay out of my area! Why are you sticking your nose in my business? Don't you have enough to do in your own ministry? You're always grabbing for more power"). This sounds like the language of the cutthroat business world, but it is also stated or implied in many church conflicts. Just as second chair leaders need a healthy relationship with their first chair, they have to build strong, trust-based relationships with peers in their organization. In the church, these peers may include others on the church staff, members of the governing board, and key lay leaders.

Cross the Line Horizontally

As we described in Chapter Four, an invisible line determines the freedom and authority for a second chair leader in relationship to the first chair. An even more subtle line defines the freedom that a second chair has in influencing peers. Some would say the line is not subtle at all; "you do your job and I'll do mine." But we define a second chair leader as someone with an organizationwide perspective and a passion to see the entire body perform at its very best. Chapelwood United Methodist had just finished a new vision statement when Bob Johnson joined the staff. Bob fully agreed with the vision but felt it should be simplified to have the greatest value to the congregation. He worked with the key lay leaders and the senior pastor to make the modifications. It would have been easier for Bob to stay quiet, but that is not what second chair leaders do. When something is less than optimal in any part of the congregation, they cannot help but be concerned.

West University Baptist is a family-oriented church. Much of our growth has come from families who first participate in one of the weekday or summer programs, such as our preschool or after-school care. They experience a warm, Christian environment and are drawn into the life of the church. During our annual sign-up period in 2003, Mike was concerned that many parents had to wait several hours to register their children for the upcoming school year. He was also concerned that we were using a paper system, even though our core constituency is highly educated and computer-savvy.

After observing this process, Mike met with Barbara Chrisman, our children's ministry director, and expressed his concerns. He offered to put his thoughts—concerns and possible solutions—in writing and review them with her and her ministry leadership team. The discussion was quite positive; we all wanted to make the process as smooth and efficient as possible. Some of Mike's suggestions were impractical, some were easy to implement, and others required expertise that the children's ministry did not possess. The following year, they implemented many of the changes and received a number of compliments from parents about the improvements.

Mike does not have any responsibility for the children's ministry, but this entire change occurred with very little resistance. Why? It started with relationships. Barbara and Mike have similar hearts for ministry and have built a strong relationship over time. She heard his initial comments not as criticism but as an honest attempt to help improve her ministry area. Mike's ideas were offered as suggestions, allowing some to be rejected and others to be modified. As we involved the rest of Barbara's team in the process, they gained ownership in the solution. The final step was for Mike to provide resources they lacked: designing a simple computer-based system for registration, borrowing computers for the two-day process, and lending the help of an administrative assistant.

It sounds simple, but too many second chair leaders become the proverbial bull in the china shop when they step into another person's ministry area. Recall the last time you tried to help someone else improve their ministry; what was the result? If the outcome was negative, if your assistance was rejected or your advice was not followed, what kept you from being successful? Our guess is that one or more of several factors prevented you from achieving your desired result:

o You did not start with a strong, trust-based relationship.

o Your attempt to help was seen as self-serving.

o The manner in which your assistance was offered was wrong—too harsh or judgmental.

o You touched on a particularly sensitive area, something in which the other person felt vulnerable or inadequate.

Trying to compel another person to accept assistance never works, especially when the person is a peer. Your ability to help a colleague is dependent on the other person's cooperation. If any of the factors in the list occurs, the supposed help can quickly degenerate into competition rather than cooperation. The person being helped views the offer with suspicion, thinking the one making the offer has a hidden agenda. Rather than seeing improvement in the effectiveness of the organization, relationships are damaged and performance slips.

How are your relationships with other staff members and key leaders in your congregation or workplace? If they are not as strong as you would like, why is this the case? One major element that undermines these relationships is a lack of time spent developing them. Bill Hybels (2002) talks about managing relationships in all directions: north, south, east, and west. Many leaders, however, are not balanced across the relational compass points. Most of their time is spent in the "north" relationship with their supervisor and in the "south" relationships with those they supervise, staff members who report to them or volunteers and lay leaders in the ministry areas for which they are responsible. The "east-west" relationships that they do emphasize are usually based on affinity or specific tasks that overlap. But what about the relations with other important leaders across the organization?

The Value of Teams

Several of the second chair leaders with whom we spoke talked at length about the close-knit, highly effective teams of which they are a part. In the remainder of this chapter, we refer to four of these individuals. Kelli Caskey is the copastor of Crossroads Community Church, Geoff Surratt is the network pastor of Seacoast Church, Dian Kidd is the associate director of Union Baptist Association (UBA), and Kim Miller is the creative director of Ginghamsburg Church. The roles of these second chair leaders differ considerably, as do the organizations in which they serve. But the existence of a strong, effective team is an essential part of each story. What are the secrets of these teams, and how have these second chairs contributed to their vitality?

Even though many second chair leaders find teams to be essential, there is no formula for the size or make-up of a team. They are as small as three or four people and as large as eight to ten. The leadership team may include vocational and volunteer leaders, as is the case at Crossroads. The composition of some of these teams remains constant over a long period, while others are more fluid. The leadership teams at both Ginghamsburg and UBA include individuals who are visionaries and those who are attuned to the operations and other details of the organization. In contrast, Geoff Surratt describes the eight-person management team at Seacoast Church as being "big-picture, ADD" type personalities, except for the business administrator.

One thing they have in common is that God has placed a bold and exciting vision in each person's heart. They are convinced the team is the only way to accomplish the vision to which God has called them. Accomplishing this vision without the help of others is simply inconceivable. Because this vision is God's, they are less concerned about personal recognition and more interested in organizational achievement. The attitude of these second chair leaders is driven by a burning desire to see the entire organization perform at its very best. Kim Miller says, "I want to see God work, and I can get excited about seeing God work anywhere in the church."

What are the other common elements of these teams? Far more important than the number of members are the underlying, less visible factors that are critical to a team's success. These second chair leaders describe their team as an environment in which collaboration, mutual dependence, and consensus in decision making are the norm. They recognize the unique and complementary gifts each team member contributes. They also acknowledge the hard work involved in fostering a team environment. They agree that "real teams do not emerge unless the individuals on them take risks involving conflict, trust, interdependence, and hard work" (Katzenbach and Smith, 1993, p. 109).

So, are teams worth the effort? What *is* a team? In *The Wisdom of Teams,* Jon Katzenbach and Douglas Smith describe the benefits and characteristics of high-performance teams. They propose a helpful distinction between real teams and groups that masquerade as teams: "In any situation requiring the real-time combination of multiple skills, experiences, and judgments, a team inevitably gets better results than a collection of individuals operating within confined job roles and responsibilities" (1993, p. 15). They also give a clear and helpful definition of a real team: "A team is a small number of people with complementary skills who are committed to a common purpose, performance goals, and approach for which they hold themselves mutually accountable" (p. 45). Their book, with its explicit definition of team, was a catalyst in the formation of the director team at UBA. This definition is also an accurate description of the composition and motivation of the other leadership teams in this chapter.

Fostering Teams from the Second Chair

A team is not simply created by an edict from the first chair. It requires the full commitment of the team members. The second chair should be a leader in making this commitment and encouraging the behavior that establishes a real team. Even without the senior leader taking the initiative to build a team, many of the benefits of this collaborative relationship can be achieved. So what is the unique role of the second chair leader in building and strengthening the team?

The Importance of Diversity

Second chair leaders who are team builders understand and value the unique gifts and perspectives that each person brings to the table. Kim Miller described three contrasting roles played by her colleagues and herself: Mike Slaughter is the visionary, Sue Nilson Kibbey is the "ultimate detail person," and Kim is attuned to the creative side and the culture of the organization. Dian Kidd of UBA says this of her team: "We know we approach things differently, and we really believe that is a good thing." Kelli Caskey was quite intentional in looking for diversity—in gifts and viewpoints—as the Crossroads leadership team was being built.

What does it mean for a team to have diversity in the gifts, abilities, and passions of its members? Think about the team (or potential team) where you serve. How do its members differ? The obvious answer relates to typical areas of functional expertise: teaching, music, arts, youth, children, and administration in a local church setting. In a denominational entity, these areas might include missions, church health, leadership development, new works, property, credentials, and finance. But think about the other dimensions that can make a team truly effective. If the team tends to spend time talking about grandiose ideas, is there a realist who asks practical implementation questions? Who can convert goals into processes and action plans? Who is attuned to the needs and moods of people on the team and in the organization? Who brings a gift of clear and concise communication? Who is the creative spark on your team? Is there someone who can take several ideas that seem to be incompatible and shape them into a single suggestion that everyone recognizes as a better solution? Who adds levity and encouragement to the group dynamic? In our team, Barbara Chrisman has an ability to identify spiritual dynamics in our church body. Mat Yelvington is able to challenge the status quo and bring fresh, creative ideas into our discussions. We would be a weaker team if they only spoke on matters related to the children's and youth ministries.

An effective team may not require all these attributes. But think about your team: which of these dynamics currently exist there, and which are missing? What is needed to move your group from a potential team to a real one? If your first reaction is "more support from our first chair," then you are missing the point. As a second chair leader, you can identify and encourage these characteristics in others. Within your current group, there may be individuals who possess these abilities but do not use them. They may respond to encouragement to see the importance of their potential contributions. As you think about the current limitations or weaknesses of your team, you may even think of other individuals who should be added to the team. Of course, this must be done with the first chair's permission. But one of your biggest contributions as a second chair leader may be to identify volunteer or staff leaders whose presence can be an important enhancement.

The need for diversity may even require you to change how you contribute to your team. When Jim Herrington was UBA's executive director, he tended to bring lots of blue-sky ideas into the director team. Dian Kidd became the practical ballast for Jim's ideas. Jim could go to the edge with his brainstorming, and Dian would bring the discussion back to the practical level. When Jim left and Tom Billings became executive director, Dian's role on the team shifted. Because Tom is more cautious and deliberate by nature, Dian needed to redefine her unique contribution to the team. This took time and open discussion between Tom and Dian, but it has ultimately allowed both of them to focus on areas of strength.

Diversity of contributions brings great value to a team, but it comes with its own challenges. How do you respond to people whose strengths and gifts differ from yours? When a detail-oriented person on the team asks a series of *how-to* questions to your big ideas, do you quietly fume and wish they would be quiet? Is there someone else who just has too much fun and can never get serious? Taken too far, either characteristic can detract from the team. But before you label such a person as disruptive or detrimental, consider the reason for your reaction. Perhaps you do not place a high enough value on diversity within your team. Consider also whether they might be saying similar things about you; maybe you are too serious or never think about the practical implications of your great ideas. The point is simple: a second chair leader sees the great benefits of diversity on a team and seeks to encourage and build this diversity.

More Than Diversity

As diversity is more valued, hierarchy becomes less important for second chair leaders. They treat others on the team as peers, regardless of the person's job title or position on the organization chart. They are keenly aware that every person on their leadership team is in a subordinate role and has the potential of being a second chair leader (except for one first chair leader). In some cases, a title may designate the person as the official number-two position in the organization: executive pastor, associate director, vice president. But their interactions with other key team members indicate an attitude of respect and cooperation, not positional authority.

Kelli Caskey, the copastor of Crossroads Church, has such a title, but she is diligent in treating others on the team more as peers and less as subordinates. Other organizations intentionally avoid having an official number-two position. Seacoast Church has had an executive pastor on two occasions, but it did not work for them. Geoff Surratt says it was "like herding cats." Instead, they now opt for a team of peers. In both models, the important lesson for second chair leaders is the attitude they display toward others on the team. It is an attitude that says, "I'm glad we're on this team together." Rank is less important than relationship. Successful cooperation is more important than winning a competition.

Valuing diversity and a nonhierarchical attitude are key characteristics for second chair leaders. So is patience. An effective team does not form overnight. Coworkers do not become genuine teammates at the simple command of the first chair leader. Although there is usually a conscious decision by the senior leader to move toward a real team, this is just the first step. The emergence of a functioning team typically occurs over months or years. It takes time to develop a deep understanding of each other's unique abilities.

This patience is not just a matter of time; it takes intentionality. Driven by a passion for their organization and a strong belief in the value of teams, these leaders make teamwork a priority by investing their time and relational energy. Time together as a team is not "just another meeting." Instead, they view it as one of the most important and productive parts of their week. They resist the urge to rush through the meeting so that they can get back to work. Retreats are a frequent and eagerly anticipated part of how they spend time together.

All of this leads to relationships between team members that are deep and healthy. Once you have worked closely with someone and know their honest desire to do their best and see the organization thrive, the relational dynamic takes on an entirely different character. If relationships are strained because of disagreement, colleagues work quickly to make things right. Many of the casual work relationships in organizations are like teen romance; they are a "match of convenience" that lasts so long as both parties are happy. The relationships in an effective team are more like a strong marriage; team members know that the game is about much more than superficial happiness, and they find ways to work through their differences. In fact, they find these disparities can make them stronger.

We (Mike and Roger) are dissimilar in many ways, and as a result we drive each other crazy at times. But we have learned to appreciate each other's strengths and offer support and grace in areas of weakness. We work behind the scenes to sort out any conflict that arises because of these differences. We frequently seek advice from one another, even if not required by our defined responsibilities.

So what is your role, second chair leader, in helping your organization make the shift to working as a team? The obvious starting point is to discuss the concept with your first chair leader. But even if he or she is not ready to make a full commitment, there are numerous steps you can take to move toward teamwork. How might you improve relations with other key leaders in the organization? Do you need to spend more time with them? Have you had past conflict that has to be resolved? Whose style and gifts are most unlike yours? What can you do to value these abilities and express your appreciation for their contribution? These actions do not require a formal "we are a team" declaration; they can be initiated unilaterally. You might look for specific learning opportunities that move your group toward becoming a true team. Reading a book such as *The Wisdom of Teams,* scheduling a retreat in which you focus on team, or participating in a team-building event can all be valuable steps.

Perhaps one or two complex, cross-organization challenges must be solved. If so, this might be a great place to begin using a more collaborative approach. If possible, choose something in an area where you have some degree of responsibility, so you can model the right collaborative attitude from the start—one that says, "This problem is bigger and more complex than I can figure out on my own. I'd like some help in thinking about possible solutions." As you do so, be sure to encourage participation from everyone in the group. Be aware of how the final solution is better than what your solo effort would have produced.

Speaking into the Organization

When a true team emerges, performance improves not because team members like each other better but because collectively they can make better decisions on the important issues facing the organization. One critical dimension is the ability of each team member to speak into any part of the organization. This is the essence of a collaborative environment. This ability to make meaningful contributions beyond your official role is central to the deep-wide paradox. Kim Miller feels free to offer input into any ministry at Ginghamsburg. Geoff Surratt says, "My job is to be a teaching pastor and to oversee the satellite campuses. My value is being able to speak into any area in the life of the church."

Why do you need a team to do this? If you are the undisputed number-two person in a hierarchical organization, you may not require the team. But for anyone else—including those in the number-two role who cooperate closely with others on the staff—the team is where learning and decision making occur. If you have an idea to improve the way your church does a ministry for which you have no direct responsibility, how should you present this idea? Going to the first chair leader is heavy-handed; asking a lay leader inside the ministry area to push for the idea is manipulative. If it is a significant concept, the best forum is within the leadership team, where the person who has responsibility for the ministry and other key leaders can all participate in the dialogue. This does not mean your proposal is assured of acceptance, but a positive team environment can determine if it is a good idea and may find ways to improve the original concept.

Too many churches and other organizations do not allow this kind of interaction. When the leaders meet, their sole purpose is to coordinate their activities and then dismiss as quickly as possible to go about their respective tasks. There is little opportunity to offer suggestions to each other or collaborate on cross-departmental issues. Katzenbach and Smith make a clear distinction between this "working group" approach and a high-performance team. The implicit model in a working group is "You do your job, I'll do mine, and the first chair leader can deal with any conflicts or major concerns." As you can see, this pushes you right back into a silo, just the place you tried to escape in the previous chapter by developing a wider perspective.

Your first reaction may be, "I'd sure like to offer some suggestions for So-and-So's area of ministry." If you are thinking this, you are missing half the point. Are you equally willing for that person to highlight potential ways to improve your area? Are you willing to be open about the challenges you are facing and invite other team members to help you develop better solutions? Do you see the necessity of collaborating with others on the major issues facing your church or organization? If not, you are not ready for truly working as a second chair leader in a team environment.

Building Your Own Teams

The second chair is a member of the senior leadership team, but he or she is often the leader of one or more other teams in the organization. Many of the principles we have already described are just as applicable for the role of team leader. These qualities of diversity, patience, intentionality, honesty, and relational vitality are no less essential for the teams you lead.

In your area of responsibility, what challenges could you meet better with a team approach? If the current results are not what you desire, would a fresh perspective or new talent make a meaningful difference? When West University Baptist wanted to take its worship service to the next level, we decided we needed some fresh ideas. We formed a "creative team" to help answer the question, "How can we improve our worship services through greater use of the arts?" Even though we are still in the early stages of making this shift, the question clearly requires a team approach. No one individual has all the knowledge, expertise, and creativity to accomplish our goal. The spark for the team is coming from several lay leaders enlisted for this specific task.

Being the team leader, though, places you in a new position and exposes you to new demands. Think about the team where you are not in charge. What would you change? Note your answer so you can do things differently in the team you lead. Start by deciding whether to encourage creation of a real team. Real teams are needed for some situations but are not necessary in others. In making this decision, ask yourself how much collaboration you want to see among the members of the group. As the team leader, you can select projects that force team members to work together closely; you can facilitate meetings to solicit contributions from everyone, or set goals that require integrated, creative solutions. You can also make the meeting perfunctory and quench the spirit of collaboration. Your role as leader is a key determinant of whether the group functions as a real team.

A second chair who leads a team also has a role when it comes to relationships among the team members. It is essential to treat team members with respect. When you as leader are trying to establish a real team, this means allowing dissent. It means allowing time for everyone to contribute ideas, and valuing those contributions. You are not just a team member; you are a person with disproportionate influence over the group's direction and decisions. How you use that influence sends important signals of respect, or lack thereof, to the rest of the team.

How disproportionate should your influence be? Will you be more of a peer or play a strong, directive role? Some of the most effective teams are led by second chairs who follow the one-millimeter principle; rather than emphasizing their authority, their actions clearly indicate that everyone is equal around the table. Dian Kidd leads the consultant team at UBA by following the same philosophy of inclusiveness and consensus that she finds on the director (leadership) team.

Finally, recognize that team dynamics are often more complicated when the composition includes staff members and volunteers. This is true in churches, judicatories, and other organizations that use volunteer leaders in their committees or other subunits. In leading this type of group, be precise about the roles that are expected of all members. If roles are not clear, people will interject assumptions to define their own jobs and their expectations of others. The gap between expectation and reality is filled with frustration. So avoid it by clarifying the group's purpose and the expectations you have for each member.

This obviously requires communication—another ingredient that is often lacking in teams, especially those that include a mix of volunteers and staff. Full-time staff members tend to communicate at a level that is appropriate and sufficient for others who are on the inside. But volunteers are not present in all the casual conversations and internal meetings. As a result, they may not have the information they require to understand and do their job. Be aware of what they have been told directly and what they should hear. Do not assume that someone has told them or that they have figured it out. Spend time *listening* to all your team members so you know what they know about any important issue.

One of Geoff Surratt's primary roles is to lead the team of campus pastors who are responsible for Seacoast's eight satellite campuses. He faces many challenges in establishing a true team among this group. Each person is, in a sense, a first chair with a full slate of responsibilities on his own campus. Furthermore, they are geographically dispersed, which prevents them from having frequent in-person meetings. The value of team, however, drives them back together. Pioneering new, more effective ways to function as one church with multiple campuses requires that they communicate and collaborate. Geoff tries to ensure that every campus pastor has a clear understanding of the Seacoast vision. A weekly conference call for all the campus pastors, periodic retreats, and frequent one-on-one conversations with Geoff are all part of the team's success.

The people and the potential teams in your areas of service are a great source of leverage. As you invest in them—through time, relationship, trust, prayer, and communication—the work that can be accomplished increases exponentially. It is a slow, one-person-at-a-time process. But the benefits for you and the organization make it all worthwhile.

Some Traps to Avoid

If building a team sounds easy, think again. Many people bring a lot of bad habits and baggage into a team environment. For some, it is insecurity about job performance. They do not really want to collaborate, because the suggestions made by others point out their mistakes and inadequacies. For others, it is an intensely competitive nature that sees everything as a zero-sum game. In this mind-set, a peer's success is viewed as "their gain and my loss." Then some simply have not spent enough time working in this type of environment to know some of the behaviors that can encourage or discourage teamwork. When you boil it down, two major traps to avoid are being overly critical of peers and doing things that are perceived as self-serving.

For example, how do you express disagreement with something another team member says during a planning meeting? Some people believe honesty is the best policy and consistently voice their perspectives—often rather bluntly. Others want to avoid any appearance of conflict and will keep their mouth shut at all costs. In truth, neither is the right answer. The best approach is situational. Some discussions can be handled offline so that the first chair and other peers are not involved. Other times, the issue is important enough that you need to speak up. It is also situational because of the specific relationships. Because we (Mike and Roger) have a strong relationship, we are both comfortable expressing opposing views around each other. We have also been in work environments where we had to be much more cautious in challenging a colleague. Whatever the case, be aware of how you communicate disagreement.

Even if you are not overly critical, you can still fall into a trap. Often the suggestions made by the person wearing a second chair hat are not *befitting* of the position, they are only *benefiting* his position. Self-promotion is lethal for teams. Second chairs should always keep the entire organization in mind. That means some recommendations will hurt their specific area or make life more difficult for themselves. Think about the last couple of major disagreements you had with someone on your team. How was your position interpreted by others? Was it seen as self-serving? Did your critique enhance your standing in the eyes of the first chair? Did it help the part of the organization for which you have direct responsibility?

You can avoid these traps by living with an awareness of their existence. You may have other tendencies that work against a positive team atmosphere. One of Mike's strengths is his strong analytical, problem-solving mind-set. As a result, he is quick to identify problems and can be seen as being too negative or always shooting down the ideas of others. When it comes to enlisting and empowering people, Roger is a step ahead of everyone. He has to guard against empowering them to the point where he is uninvolved or they are not accountable for a certain level of results. Each of these, as described, is the negative side of a positive trait. Whatever your tendencies, be aware of how they affect your team.

Here are some practical steps for avoiding the traps that undermine teamwork:

- *Be selective.* It is not necessary to have a comment or opinion on every issue, especially if your natural tendency is to be critical. Be especially careful around those with whom you have not established a strong working relationship.

- *Be affirming.* The two-to-one principle is helpful: offer two positive and encouraging comments for every one criticism. If encouragement is not your natural temperament, this is all the more reason to make it a regular habit.

○ *Be unselfish.* Think about the needs of the organization and your coworkers. Be sure your recommendations are not always benefiting you.

○ *Be discreet.* If you have a choice, save the negative comments for an offline, one-on-one meeting. Before you tell the entire staff about a mistake that was made by a colleague, ask yourself if there is any reason this needs to be voiced in front of everyone.

○ *Be constructive.* Learn how to say, "Yes, *and* . . ." in discussions rather than "Yes, *but* . . ." The latter indicates disagreeing with the idea, while the former is an affirming way to build on a colleague's positive suggestion.

○ *Be involved.* The team is not something to be delegated. Involvement enables you to do all the other things listed here. It keeps you in close relationship so that your praises and critiques are interpreted correctly.

In truth, much of your ability to achieve your full potential as a second chair leader does not depend on title or position; it depends on the voluntary cooperation of coworkers and other constituents in the organization. If they see you putting self first, they begin to withdraw this authority. If they see you building your own empire—and putting on a pretense of sacrifice or humility—they will not be there for you in the future. On the other hand, as they experience you being genuine in your concern for them and the church they are much more willing to support you.

The Second Chair as Servant Leader

The preceding discussion listed some actions and attitudes that a second chair leader must avoid if he or she wants to build a strong team. The chemistry of an effective team is catalyzed by one final concept: "servant leadership." This is the title of Robert Greenleaf's classic book on the subject. More important, it is the clear teaching of Jesus: "Whoever wants to become great among you must be your servant, and whoever wants to be first must be slave of all" (Mark 10:43–44).

The second chair leader who wants to thrive, personally and organizationally, builds a team by exhibiting a servant's heart. Greenleaf says it well: "A new moral principle is emerging which holds that the only authority deserving one's allegiance is that which is freely and knowingly granted by the led to the leader in response to, and in proportion to, the clearly evident servant stature of the leader. Those who choose to follow this principle will not casually accept the authority of existing institutions. *Rather, they will freely respond only to individuals who are chosen as leaders because they are proven and trusted as servants"* (Greenleaf, 1997, p. 10).

If you are a second chair leader, you are in the spotlight. Peers and others in the organization are aware of your actions and attitudes. Do they see you as someone who wants to be noticed? Do you have a reputation for being too important to be bothered with small matters, or one for rolling up your sleeves and doing mundane jobs? The decision to be a servant is entirely up to you. Unlike becoming a team, which requires mutual commitment, your peers cannot prevent you from having a servant's heart or from genuinely offering your support.

Be careful not to do it with an ulterior motive. If you start keeping score ("I'll be a servant today, so that I can help fix another part of the organization tomorrow"), you are not really serving; you are manipulating. Your service needs to come from a genuine belief that it is the right thing to do, and that the organization is better as a result. Any second chair can be a better leader by developing a "how can I help you?" attitude. As you seek ways to help, you find yourself filling any number of gaps. The practical aspects are the final chapter of the deep-wide paradox.

7

PUTTING IT INTO PRACTICE

BEING DEEP AND WIDE is not just a theory or even a good children's church song. Being deep and wide is the essence of how second chair leaders spend their time. It is the means by which they fulfill their God-given potential. So, what does this mean in practice?

We were not surprised that many second chair leaders talked about the importance of being flexible in their job. As we have already seen, a static job description is impractical for a second chair. Glenn Smith says, "You've got to be a generalist. You can't be a specialist, unless you're a specialist in flexibility." If you see the big picture and define your role as whatever is best for the organization, your specific duties are certain to change over time.

They may be generalists, but second chair leaders must be deep in some areas. This may be clearly defined by job title or job description. Robin Smith, worship leader at Farmers Branch Church of Christ, knows that God has wired him to be a visionary leader and have influence throughout the organization. At the same time, he is an accomplished musician and worship leader. Using these specific gifts is a vital part of his ministry. At times he felt limited by first chairs who wanted him to stay deep and narrow, focusing only on music. Despite these restrictions, Robin has never wanted to forsake music and worship in pursuit of being wide. Simply stated, an effective second chair leader must demonstrate depth and competence in his assigned ministry. The respect and credibility that come from using his gifts form the platform from which Robin can extend his leadership influence.

A second chair leader can also be deep in ways that do not fit a typical job description. Glenn Smith says, "Most executive pastors like to have something that's a focus, at least for a season." One of Glenn's strengths is initiating, taking the kernel of an idea and cultivating it into a program in full bloom. Shortly after his arrival, Glenn launched a leadership development program at Sugar Creek. Once it was up and running, he initiated a church planting movement that has led to thirty-six new works in five years.

Depth for other second chair leaders is seen in their troubleshooting abilities. They are known to their first chairs and the rest of the organization as the person who can be counted on to solve even the most difficult problems. Their success may be derived from keen insight, creative thinking, and a motivational touch. Whatever the specific skills and techniques, they get the job done. When Bob Johnson came to Chapelwood United Methodist as executive pastor, he was immediately given one of these assignments. Under Senior Pastor Jim Jackson, the church has made a major shift to become lay-led. A key part of this strategy is the design of Chapelwood's Council on Ministries. This is a coordinating, planning, and decision-making body that includes more than fifty laypeople and a dozen or so staff members. They represent six "purposes" and seven "relational areas" in the church. These two dimensions form a grid around which the council is structured. This grid looks complicated on paper, and it was proving unwieldy in practice, so Bob was assigned to evaluate this structure and if possible make it work to harness the congregation's capable lay leaders. His abilities to organize, pay attention to detail, and work with people are vital as the council is becoming a much more effective body for mobilization of the laity.

Then there are times when you are expected to be deep in areas for which you have not been trained or gifted at all. Most second chair leaders do not have the luxury of telling the first chair, "I don't think I should do this task. It's really not what I do well." If they do, they should be prepared for the first chair to give them a Nike answer: "Just do it!" Rather than escaping, you should look at these as opportunities to grow personally, develop new skills, and help the organization. When Roger moved from the role of student minister to associate pastor, he assumed responsibility for budget planning and administration. Even though he would rather preach a sermon (or even sweep the floor) than pore over a page of numbers, he accepted it as part of the job and a learning opportunity. He spent extra time on the financials and sought help to improve his skills in this area. He is a stronger and more versatile leader as a result.

Four Practices

A second chair leader might need to be deep in any number of areas, and it is beyond our scope to address them all. In the remainder of this chapter, however, we look at four *practices* that can make you deeper and wider as a leader:

1. *Be a pulse taker.* Knowing what others are thinking and feeling is valuable information for you and the first chair. Your role places you in a unique position to keep a finger on the pulse of the organization.

2. *Be a vision amplifier.* The first chair is the primary vision caster in the organization, but a second chair leader has many opportunities to repeat, clarify, and reinforce the vision.

3. *Be a leader multiplier.* For the second chair, identifying and recruiting other leaders who can help achieve the vision should be an ongoing priority.

4. *Be a gap filler.* If there is no other leader who can serve in a critical role, the second chair should be prepared to fill the gap.

Be a Pulse Taker

Think of the last time your church faced a major decision. Did you and other leaders feel anxious not knowing whether the congregation would support the recommendation? Every organization has pivotal moments of decision, a time when a clear consensus is needed to move forward. But in the period leading up to the decision, it is sometimes unclear if a consensus will be reached.

Taking the pulse means assessing the organization's attitude toward a change or important decision. In many churches, the senior pastor has the worst seat in the house when it comes to pulse taking. Many members do not tell him what they are really thinking. You may not be sure about those that do; are they chronic complainers? Or are they saying what they think the first chair wants to hear? A second chair leader is often in a better position to truly hear what others are thinking. She may also be more neutral in listening. After all, if the first chair has taken a firm and visible stand, it may be hard for him to hear criticism without reacting to it. The first chair may want to offer a rebuttal, but the second chair may be able to discern the speaker's real issue. At the very least, the second chair leader has her own network of relationships, different from that of the first chair.

Kelli Caskey of Crossroads Community was a pulse taker when the church was given the opportunity to realize its dream. Guy Caskey, the senior pastor and Kelli's husband, wanted to have a large coffeehouse for their primary worship venue. Reaching "the pierced, painted, and professional" community, as Guy felt called to do, required a nonthreatening, relational environment. When a four-thousand-square-foot coffeehouse was made available for Sunday mornings, the leadership team's immediate reaction was "yes!" But there were many details to be resolved, not the least of which was the question of space for children. Crossroads was then meeting on Saturday evenings in a borrowed church with separate rooms for children. Because the new facility was going to be a coffeehouse for six and a half days a week, the only dedicated children's space would be a small nursery area.

No one wanted to step away from this opportunity, and many were hesitant to voice their concerns. After all, Guy had been talking and dreaming about it for years. But Kelli and other leaders could feel the uneasiness in the congregational pulse, and they realized a solution for children was essential. As the leadership team searched for ideas, they concluded that a new worship service was the best answer. The result—a creative, highly interactive family worship service—enabled Crossroads to move into the coffeehouse while being sensitive to families.

One specific aspect of pulse taking is spotting organizational wildfires. For several of our second chair interviewees, a firm rule governing their relationship with the first chair is "no surprises." The senior pastor does not want to be ambushed by an angry member on Sunday morning. The synod executive should be told about a problem *before* the phone rings. As the second chair, it is your job to give this advance warning whenever possible. The issue may have been beyond your control or it may be of your own making. If the latter, this means taking personal responsibility: "I've made a mistake, and you're going to be hearing about it." If the former, you do not have to take the blame, but you still need to alert the first chair. Either way, the ultimate consequences of not giving advance notice are worse than those of bringing an unwelcome message.

"No surprises" requires you to know about the surprise ahead of time. Are you well connected within your organization? Just because you are a second chair leader does not mean you have a broad relational network. How much time do you spend talking with people? How much of this time is spent asking questions and listening (as opposed to recruiting or convincing)? If you are a church leader, how do you spend your time during the limited hours when the congregation gathers? Have you developed the ability to discern the difference between an isolated gripe and a broader feeling of dissatisfaction? Or the difference between one enthusiastic supporter and a general consensus?

Effective second chair leaders are in the information business. Even if they have a clear sense of God's direction, they have to know if the rest of the organization is following. They understand that accurate information is essential for making the right decision at the right time. They can listen and ask questions. They gather information accurately. They determine what information is important and what is not. They are able to communicate this information to their first chair and to others who need to know.

In the end, being a pulse taker can also place you as a second chair leader in a difficult position. You may be the one who hears negative comments that should be reported to the first chair or the leadership team. Robin Smith describes the challenge of "truth telling with graciousness," but he quickly explains, "If I've earned trust, I'm able to say hard things." This does not mean every negative comment must be repeated to the first chair. The decision depends on the ground rules for your relationship and your assessment of the significance of the comment.

Even with a hands-off first chair, there are times when you are the bearer of bad news. How do you keep your boss from shooting the messenger? First, keep in mind that you are not just a messenger; you are a leader. But you are a leader who is expected to show loyalty to your first chair. The tone and timing of your message are extremely important. If your words indicate that you lack loyalty, you have gone beyond pulse taking. Ric Hodgin, of the A.D. Players, says that as a second chair leader you are "always walking the line of being 100 percent supportive of the one person above you, dealing with the needs of everyone below, and making these match." Others might decide to jump on the bandwagon when they hear the negatives, but you must make an unequivocal commitment to the organization and the first chair, even as you are taking the pulse. In a sense, you are just a messenger when you play the role of pulse taker, but a second chair's deep and wide responsibilities do not stop here.

Be a Vision Amplifier

Every time you listen, you have an opportunity to communicate. In taking the pulse, you also have a chance to influence the pulse. What do you do with those opportunities? When someone complains to you about a major shift in your church, what is your response? Every significant conversation with another leader or other constituent is an opportunity to help that person understand the vision. If she is questioning a decision, can you show the connection between the decision and the vision? If she has *why* questions, can they be answered in the context of the vision?

What happens when an older member complains about a shortage of parking spaces at church? You might sympathize and tell him you are sorry for any inconvenience. You might agree that it is a growing problem and tell him you will get to the bottom of the situation. Or you might respectfully explain that God is blessing the church's commitment to evangelism and that more unbelievers are coming to worship on Sundays. In doing so, you might also encourage him to continue to pray that these visitors will be transformed into devoted followers of Christ. Only this last answer promotes amplification of the vision.

Of course, this requires that you have a clear understanding of the vision first. The ability to recite a vision statement does not equate with understanding; the ability to describe the vision and its implications does. Even in-depth understanding is not enough for second chair leaders. They need to be fully committed to the vision and how the organization is trying to follow it. Said another way, you cannot amplify what you do not agree with or understand. Just like a bad loudspeaker on a stereo system, the leader who is not on board will distort rather than amplify the vision.

This reactive role—responding to questions and comments—is just the start of being a vision amplifier. As second chair, you must be proactive in helping other leaders understand and implement the organization's vision. This is especially true in the areas for which you are directly responsible. What are you doing to clarify vision for those who follow you? Have you spent time exploring the implications of the vision for each of them? Every time another leader takes hold of the vision, the organization's potential to achieve grows exponentially. It is exciting when your team members begin to truly catch the vision and take personal ownership of it.

Sometimes you amplify the vision by bringing it to life, by putting flesh on the skeleton of an idea. When Greg Surratt, senior pastor of Seacoast Church, first envisioned a multisite approach, it was a typical big-picture idea that still needed the supporting details. Being a multisite church was not part of the Seacoast vision statement or culture at the time, but reaching the lost was at the core of the congregation's values. Greg knew a second campus would relieve Seacoast's space constraints, and he believed it would also accelerate evangelistic outreach. So Greg turned to his brother, Geoff, who was already on the Seacoast staff, and asked him to take the multisite idea from concept to fruition. At first Geoff was skeptical, but he and a key lieutenant continued to develop the idea. Before long, they were convinced that a second campus was more than possible; it was an exciting part of God's plan for Seacoast. A little over two years later, Seacoast now worships on nine campuses and continues to expand. As network pastor, Geoff is in the center of this plan, the chief amplifier of a concept that has redefined Seacoast Church.

Some second chairs may even be given a unique custodial responsibility related to the vision. A strong sense for the vision enables them to play a key role in keeping the vision in front of the entire organization. This is normally the job of the first chair, but consider the case of Kim Miller. Of the six people on the leadership team, Kim has the strongest sense of the "Ginghamsburg DNA." As a result, she composes most of the letters, public relations pieces, and other communications for the church, regardless of whose signature appears on the document. She oversees many of the visual aspects of the church, from worship planning to design of the physical spaces on the campus. This requires an incredibly strong shared vision among the leadership team, but it also yields a great benefit in the consistency of the message that is communicated at Ginghamsburg.

Vision is also full of challenges. At the top level, a vision almost always sounds exciting. Down in the details, difficult choices must be made. Second chairs who amplify the vision should be willing to roll up their sleeves as they pursue its call. Preston Mitchell, of Fellowship Church says, "The reality is that the second chair gets dirty sometimes. I do it to free up the leader to be the vision person." When the time comes to protect or promote the vision, what do you do? You might be the one who has to cancel a program because priorities have changed. You might need to ask a leader to step aside. Even these difficult tasks can amplify the vision if they are done correctly.

In the third paradox, we discuss how your dreams intersect with the vision of the first chair. For now, our hope is that you are part of a great organization with a great vision, and that you consider it a joy to be a vision amplifier.

Be a Leader Multiplier

When Robin Smith was called to the position of associate worship minister at Oak Hills Church in San Antonio, he knew it would be an exciting and challenging opportunity. He was working for two high-profile, highly respected leaders: Max Lucado, senior minister, and Jeff Nelson, who is seen as the "grandfather of worship music" among Church of Christ leaders. Robin's primary role was to build an instrumental worship program at Oak Hills. This was a new direction for the church because of its denominational background. Robin feels deeply that church leaders should be multiplying themselves by preparing others to take their places. This is not an ego-driven belief; it is a humble and genuine desire that the church be stronger because of his influence, a determination to "invest myself in something that outlives me."

When Robin arrived, Oak Hills had one praise band. As he continued to serve, the number of bands grew, and Robin focused his energy on cultivating leaders from within each. After just three years, Oak Hills had five bands, four of which were being led by people Robin had recruited and mentored. When Robin left, Max Lucado praised Robin for his success in cultivating other leaders at Oak Hills.

As you amplify the vision, you become aware of people who are excited about this direction and who appear to have great leadership potential. You also see that a God-given vision requires a growing base of leaders, and you know of some of the organization's specific leadership needs. What do you do with the knowledge? If you are a leader multiplier, you start playing matchmaker. You learn more about the specific interests of these potential leaders, and you think about places they might serve. You test their capabilities and commitment in apprenticeship. Ultimately, you release and empower them so you can continue the multiplication process.

When our church decided to build more creativity into our worship services, we did not have the budget to hire a creative director. Instead, we turned to Tony Gray, who was clearly enthusiastic about using videos, drama, and other creative elements. At first, Tony helped with specific, short-term assignments. All were done well, and Tony continued to come back with more ideas. We learned he was dependable, and we built a positive working relationship. As Tony proved himself, he quickly became a key volunteer leader in our worship ministry. What was the starting point? It was a second chair, in this case Roger, listening to Tony and identifying him as the person who could help us take a major step forward.

Sometimes multiplication is done with leaders who are already in place. Rather than recruiting additional leaders, a second chair can expand a ministry by tapping into the underused potential of its existing people. Steve Ahlquist joined North Coast Church as executive director of ministry resources, a position created by splitting the executive pastor role into two positions. This allowed Charlie Bradshaw, executive pastor, to concentrate on all the ministry functions, while Steve took on the facilities, human resource, accounting, technology, and other back-office functions. One of Steve's first actions was to create a "resource team" with the department heads who reported to him. Prior to this, the only regular team at North Coast was composed of the ministry department heads. Steve's simple decision was an important step in communicating the importance of the behind-the-scenes people, and it created a renewed sense of purpose and commitment for the group. Any time this kind of renewal takes place, the organization experiences a multiplication benefit as the level of energy and productivity grows.

Every organization has people who are not maximizing their potential. This is especially true in churches, where many "unvolunteers" sit on the sidelines, waiting to be asked and matched with the right opportunity. We make excuses about why more people are not involved—they are too busy, they are fickle, they would not be interested in this job. But we do not make it a focused priority to get them into the game. The ultimate purpose of multiplication is not the happiness of these potential leaders. It is a matter of stewardship, of affecting the Kingdom as much as possible with the people resources entrusted to each of us.

Christian leaders often quote Proverbs 29:18—"without vision the people perish." But it might be equally true to say that without leadership opportunities people lose interest in the vision. Second chair leaders can translate a wide vision into deep opportunity for new leaders.

Be a Gap Filler

Of all the ideas we discussed with our second chair interviewees, the one that resonated most deeply was the concept of being a gap filler. Most of these leaders talked about job descriptions that changed frequently and assignments that were full of variety. When Tom Billings was the associate director at Union Baptist Association, the running joke was that his job description was rewritten every twelve months. Simply stated, when an important job needs to be tackled in a dynamic organization, the first chair looks for a trusted second chair to get it done.

Greg Hawkins says the second chair leader is the "ultimate utility player." Greg has certainly fit this description: "I've been interim leader of just about every ministry at Willow Creek." He has directly led the adult, youth, small-group, and operations departments for interim periods ranging from six months to more than a year. His gap filling has also placed him in key temporary roles, such as being the point person for one of the church's capital campaigns. In fact, he expects that at least 25 percent of his time in any year will be spent in some sort of temporary, gap-filling role.

Gap filling is often a function of the first chair's strengths and weaknesses. No one excels in all areas of leadership. Whatever the first chair's weaknesses may be, the strongest and most effective organization is created when the second chairs can offset these gaps. Of course, this requires a good relationship between first and second chairs. It requires first chairs who recognize their weaknesses and are glad to have someone offset them. Bob Johnson has this kind of relationship with Jim Jackson. Jim is a remarkably innovative leader, but structure and organizational details are not his interests. These are areas in which Bob excels, though. The key to their partnership is that Jim is not threatened by someone who is gifted in the areas where he is not. Without this, Bob's ability to lead and Chapelwood's ministry impact would be diminished.

Complementing a first chair may play to the specific strengths of a second chair, or it may cause them to stretch and bend in new ways. Jim Herrington, former executive director of Union Baptist Association, is a highly intuitive, visionary leader. When Tom Billings, the current executive director, was in a second chair role, he intentionally downplayed his own intuitive nature because this was Jim's strength. Instead, he spent more time "doing charts and graphs" and other detailed tasks. This was not something that energized Tom, but it filled an important gap.

Is gap filling something second chairs are dragged into, a necessary evil that is just part of their jobs? Not at all; filling gaps often seems to stimulate a second chair. This is clearly true with Bob Johnson, and even Tom Billings found great satisfaction in playing a key role in a vibrant organization. Second chair gap fillers like the variety that comes with the change in assignment. They are excited about the challenge of working on something that few others can do well. They know they will be stronger leaders from what they learn as they delve deeply into a specific part of the organization. Their commitment to the organization pushes them to do whatever is necessary for its success.

Of course, you do not have to wait for your first chair to push you into a gap. Gap filling is the ultimate deep part of the paradox, but it is made possible by the wide perspective of the second chair leader. As you keep the big picture in mind, you may be the first person (or the only person) to see a gap. Think about the critical weaknesses in your organization. Who else is aware of these gaps? Who has a clear understanding of how they should be addressed? For example, you may be the one who realizes that your district has a poor track record in developing and retaining staff. If you are aware, it is likely you have a head start on a solution. Or perhaps the written information from your church is always designed for insiders, leaving new and fringe members in the dark. Even if you are not responsible for communications, you can be the one to raise the issue and help make the necessary changes. The second chair leader may not be the only person to notice problems like these, but it requires a second chair attitude to take ownership and do something about them. A second chair is not content to say, "That's not my problem. I'll let someone else deal with it." Within our staff, we have a saying: "You brought it up; now deal with it!" This is the ultimate expression of second chair gap filling.

Even if you tend not to pay attention to the details, you can still be a gap filler. Every organization has gaps. No church or judicatory has fulfilled its

God-given potential. Having a clear understanding of the vision and spending time listening to others in the organization will make you aware of gaps. Make a periodic habit of asking, "How can we improve our effectiveness as an organization?" Think about the biggest, most significant obstacles that keep your ministry from advancing. Ask yourself and your team, "What keeps us from going to the next level?" The answers to these questions begin to point you toward the gaps to be filled. As you do so, your knowledge of the organization grows, your leadership toolkit expands, and your organization reaps the benefits.

Words of Caution

Each of the four practices comes with a risk of overuse or abuse. Second chair leaders must be aware of these dangers and guard against them.

Any medical professional will tell you that a person's pulse is only one indicator of health. The pulse taker in the church should avoid making sweeping generalities on the basis of a single comment. It is not right to say, "I've had several people express concern about . . ." unless you have really heard this from four or five people. One opponent, no matter how vocal, does not constitute a mandate. Did you know that one can mistakenly feel one's own pulse when trying to check the heart rate of a patient? Beware. If you already have a strong point of view, you may listen selectively for others who agree with your opinions. If you are not always testing your assumptions and beliefs against all the information you have received, you are not an adequate pulse taker.

What vision are you amplifying? A vision statement may leave lots of room for interpretation. What do you do if specificity is lacking? As second chair, you must not use this vagueness to promote a personal agenda. A vision amplifier should not be a vision redirector. A second chair's communication of the vision should be completely true to the full intent of the vision. Anything less confuses the organization and damages your relationship with the first chair. When a rock is thrown into a pond, the ripples spread across the surface of the water. If a second rock is thrown in the same place, it reinforces the ripples. But if it is thrown in another place, the ripples can cancel out as they come together. This is the challenge of vision amplification. If you are unsure about the vision, clarify before you communicate.

Leader multipliers must make sure they are developing leaders who are committed to following Christ and serving the church. The risk in leader multiplication occurs if these new leaders are primarily loyal to the second chair who recruited and cultivated them. An organization that is personality-driven may succeed so long as the dynamo leaders are in place but may quickly collapse after a leadership transition occurs. In the worst case, inappropriate multiplication can result in a church where members are divided by allegiance to various staff members or lay leaders. Remember Paul's rebuke to the church in Corinth: "For since there is jealousy and quarreling among you, are you not worldly? Are you not acting like mere men? For when one says, 'I follow Paul,' and another, 'I follow Apollos,' are you not mere men? What, after all, is Apollos? And what is Paul? Only servants through whom you came to believe—as the Lord has assigned to each his task" (1 Corinthians 3:3–5). You can offset the risk by keeping your focus on God and keeping the first chair informed and involved in leadership multiplication.

Some second chairs define their entire role on the basis of gap filling. They define themselves with a hero or martyr complex—a hero for saving the day (once again) or a martyr for being the only person who can bear the many burdens of the organization. They envision gaps where none exist, just so they can have a problem to solve. Or they rush to fill a real gap rather than looking for other leaders as the first resort. Gaps should be filled, but the second chair is not always the person to be the gap filler. So be warned: there are always more gaps to be filled. Be strategic in choosing which ones must be addressed immediately, and which ones you personally need to fill.

Deep and Wide Lay Leaders

The second chair is not reserved solely for vocational staff members, and the deep-wide paradox is a natural place for lay leaders to excel. You do not have to be in a paid staff role to see the big picture. Information may be limited if you are not on the inside, but volunteer leaders have the advantage of not being dragged down into operational minutiae. Instead, they are able to make strategic contributions in areas for which they are uniquely suited. We can illustrate this by describing the roles and contributions of two second chair lay leaders at West University Baptist.

Bobby O'Neal has been the church treasurer for more than thirty years. We have known treasurers in other churches who were stereotypical bean counters, simply making sure all the receipts and expenditures were properly accounted for. Others played the part of the watchdog, the member who makes sure that the staff does not do anything inappropriate or unauthorized with the church's money. Bobby, on the other hand, embodies both ends of the deep-wide paradox. He is gifted when it comes to the financial details and has shepherded the church through a variety of major financial decisions. When we needed to secure a major loan for a construction project, our bankers were highly complimentary about the state of our financial records and of Bobby's command of the information. But Bobby also has a clear understanding of the church's vision, and he is committed to helping us achieve it. When unanticipated needs arise, Bobby's response is, "Let's see how we can pay for this." This is in stark contrast to the watchdog attitude: "It's not in the budget. You'll just have to wait until next year." Because Bobby melds his strong financial capability with a clear sense of vision, our congregation's resources are used more effectively for God's kingdom.

Harry Craig is another second chair leader at West University Baptist. Unlike Bobby, who has had one key responsibility for years, Harry has served in a variety of roles in the church. Because of his tenure and stature, he is a key leader in pulse taking and vision amplification. But Harry's greatest contribution is in filling gaps. When we need a lay leader for a critical assignment, Harry's name is always at the top of the list. As a result, he has cochaired two strategic planning efforts in the last five years and a capital fundraising campaign in between the two. The great respect that our congregation has for Harry, his broad leadership skills, and his willingness to accept major assignments make him an invaluable person to step into the gaps.

If you are a layperson, we hope that you will recognize your potential as a second chair leader. Review the ideas in this chapter and think about how they apply to the role you play in your church. If you are in a paid staff role, think about volunteers who might be like Bobby or Harry. How should you invest in them? Do they have talents and contributions you are overlooking? As we have said from the outset, second chair leadership is not about position; it is about an attitude and an influence that are felt throughout the organization.

Are you a deep-and-wide second chair leader? Do you have a tendency toward one side of the paradox or the other? An exciting aspect of the deep-wide paradox is that you have a great deal of control over your own development. Who is to keep you from thinking about the big picture? What prevents you from developing strong relationships with peers and team members? Have you already thought of a gap that should be filled? Begin to grow deeper and wider today!

A WORD TO FIRST CHAIRS
ON THE DEEP-WIDE PARADOX

A KEY QUESTION facing first chair leaders is this: Do you truly want your second chair leaders to be deep *and* wide? The deep part is easy. Of course, you want your staff (vocational or volunteer) to do exceptional work in their specific tasks, and you want them to do more than the official job description. It sounds great to have someone whose actions match those described in Chapter Seven. Every first chair wishes for one or more supporters who truly understand the vision and help to spread it, or a respected colaborer whose identification and cultivation of other leaders allows the organization to grow stronger and more effective.

Then there is the gap filler. It sounds like a dream come true to have the ultimate utility player on your team, someone whose attitude is "Put me in the game, Coach—I'll play any position you want me to play." If their capabilities match their attitude, you are sure to have a winning team, and your job is much easier. Whatever the next challenge may be, you have the solution at your side, ready and waiting.

What is there not to like? This kind of depth and flexibility, however, comes at a cost: allowing second chair leaders to participate in the big picture—to be wide. This level of involvement implies much more than telling them what the vision is or coordinating priorities in a meeting. Participating in the big picture means allowing them to ask questions, challenge assumptions, and suggest alternatives. It means thinking of your second chair more as a partner or colleague, and less as a subordinate.

Think about a second chair in your church or business. Assume that her loyalty and commitment are not in question, and that you have a positive relationship. Can you, as first chair, imagine presenting a major new strategy and your second chair not agreeing? The disagreement is not disrespectful or personal; it is just a different perspective on the best course of action. In the right context, this clash of ideas can be healthy and productive. But some first chairs get a knot in the stomach as they think about second chairs with this much liberty and boldness. Their idea of loyalty is someone who always does what he or she is told and whose only questions are to seek clarification. This may sound safer, but it is not the description of a second chair leader. It is not consistent with the deep-wide paradox. It will not lead to the best results for your organization.

You may be thinking, "I know that a top-down style won't work. But I don't think I'm equipping my second chairs to become deep and wide."

If you are ready to release your second chairs to take their leadership to the next level, then consider these ways of teaching them.

Expand Their Thinking

Some of your potential second chair leaders may not be able to see the big picture without help. A rising leader may show great potential but only think about issues from one perspective: "How will this affect me and my ministry?" Do not assume that this person is self-centered; maybe he genuinely does not understand the bigger picture. If you think he is unable or unwilling to be a team player, you will tend to exclude him from key decisions. If the real problem is lack of understanding, it is essential to include him in those important times of decision making. You should spend extra time explaining why the chosen course of action is best. Every time you do this, you help a second chair develop a more complete perspective. You might even make a deal with him: "You are free to ask questions about a decision. In return, I expect your full support when the decision is finalized."

For example, Mike had no prior experience on a church staff before coming to West University. Roger had spent several years on church staffs but had not been in a second chair role until he became associate pastor. Our senior pastor, Barry Landrum, allows both of us to ask questions and understand the basis for his decisions. As he does that, we grow in our effectiveness as second chair leaders. It takes time and energy for all of us, but the result is well worth the effort.

Explanation is not the only way to help your second chair see the big picture more clearly. Encourage the person to reflect on a situation by asking questions that expand her thinking. For example, a group of lay leaders may be lobbying for a change in the style of worship. Ask your second chair what implications this change might have. If she says it will enable the church to reach more people in the community, ask some follow-up questions to understand her rationale and push her thinking to the next level: "Why do you think we will be able to reach more people by making this change? Can we reach the same people by doing something less disruptive? How do you think the rest of the congregation will react if we change our worship style? If we start reaching more people, what other changes will be needed to disciple them and integrate them into this congregation?" These questions and many others you could ask are designed to help the second chair see the bigger picture. This kind of reflection is a powerful way for a growing leader to learn the complexities of decision making at the top.

As a first chair leader, your time is valuable. You may feel you do not have the extra time available to explain decisions and expand a second chair's thinking. You certainly do not have the time to do so with everyone in the organization. But for those who truly are second chair leaders (or potential ones), the time is an investment with a high return. The more your second chair leaders see the big picture, the more you can release them to a significant leadership role and have confidence in the outcome.

Encourage *Real* Teams

In all likelihood, your second chair leaders found the concepts in Chapter Six appealing. If they have a sense of the broad needs of the organization, they also have a desire to improve its effectiveness. Beyond doing their own job with excellence, the best way they can contribute to the organization is through a collaborative, team-based approach.

How do you manage those who work directly for you? What happens when your staff comes together for a time of planning? Think about the communication in those meetings. Does it follow a hub-and-spoke pattern, with you at the center and the meeting consisting of a series of one-on-one conversations between you and your direct reports? Or think about the major initiatives that are undertaken by your staff. Are most of them delegated to one staff member who reports back to you with results? If this is descriptive of your environment, your staff is not functioning as a real team. If they are not experiencing true teamwork at this level, they are probably not encouraging it elsewhere in the organization.

As we described, a real team can take your ministry to the next level. But count the costs before you decide to embrace the concept. As Katzenbach and Smith explain, teams are less efficient than working groups. Think back to the communication pattern in your meetings. If you replace the hub-and-spoke with a spider web, in which every point touches every other point, the amount of interaction increases dramatically. In discussing an issue in one person's ministry, others on the team will want to chime in. The benefit is better communication, improved decisions, and greater commitment to the decisions that are made. To gain this, you have to endure some unproductive tangents and longer meetings.

The greater cost, however, is releasing some of your control over the direction of the organization. If you make a commitment to become a team, you are inviting your second chairs to take a much larger role in key decisions. You are saying you want to hear their opinions and recommendations and are open to changing your mind with their input. You are acknowledging that you do not have all the answers, and that you want help in sorting through complex decisions. If you are a Lone Ranger type of leader, this may be a difficult change.

Count the cost before you decide to encourage real teams. But before you decide it is not worth the cost, envision the gains as well. The experience from many churches and businesses around the country is that the price paid to build teams leads to tremendous benefits. They make better decisions. They work together more closely. They see new opportunities that might otherwise be overlooked. Leadership groups that learn how to function as a team thrive, in their relationships and their performance.

Foster a Stimulating Environment

One characteristic that seems to make second chair leaders distinct is their desire for variety at work. We are not talking about minor changes in their daily routine; we are talking about job descriptions that are rewritten every six months. In fact, *job description* hardly fits for them because their roles are so dynamic. They are the ones whose eyes light up when you say, "I have a challenging project, and I'm hoping you will help out."

With this in mind, what are you doing to keep your second chair leaders energized? How often do you change their assignments or ask them to solve major organizational issues? This is what they are looking for. Better yet, do not just assign a new project; discuss the areas of ministry or special projects that they might be interested in tackling. You may think it will lead to anarchy if you let everyone choose what they want to do—and you are right. But we are not talking about everyone, and we are not talking about someone writing his or her own job description. We are talking about second chair leaders pointing to the specific ways in which they can spend part of their time to add more value to the organization.

We (Mike and Roger) have both benefited from this kind of stimulating environment. Both of us have duties we carry out regularly, but we also experience great variety in our roles from week to week and month to month. We have played key leadership roles in strategic planning, construction projects, spiritual growth and capital stewardship campaigns, technology upgrades, and evangelistic emphases. These have all been special assignments in areas where we had interest and the ability to make a difference. The guiding principle for our staff is to get the essential things done, and then one is free to take initiative in other areas.

For as long as your organization is growing or changing, new needs and challenges will arise. Let your second chair leaders find specific ways of helping with these new opportunities. Give them freedom and variety to accomplish more than what their official job requires. In doing so, you encourage them and will see the performance of your organization improve.

In *How to Thrive in Associate Staff Ministry,* Kevin Lawson reports, "The associate staff members I surveyed and interviewed identified two aspects of their positions as helping them thrive . . . a dynamic position description [and] . . . input in the church's broader ministry" (2000, pp. 58–59). This is the basic challenge for first chairs who want to produce deep and wide second chair leaders. It is a challenge that is worth taking.

CONTENTMENT-DREAMING

THE THIRD PARADOX, contentment-dreaming, reaches deep down inside each of us. It stirs up a restless tension in our souls. It makes us wonder if it is possible to dream great dreams and be content at the same time. Some people escape from this tension by running to one end of the paradox or the other. One person might be pushed beyond contentment to complacency, thinking that dreams are only for dreamers or first chair leaders who can control their future. Another person is wound tighter than a spring, intent on seeing her dreams realized *now*! Yet another tries to mentally escape from his current reality, spending all of his time dreaming about the future rather than dealing in the present. Effective second chair leaders understand and live with the tension of contentment-dreaming. They know they must avoid these traps. Rather than crumpling in the tension, they let it drive them toward God, toward a determination to capture the impossible dreams that He has given them for their own lives and their ministry.

Early in life, Joseph could have been a poster boy for the society of dreamers with their head in the clouds. In Genesis 37:19, Joseph's brothers saw him approaching and said, "Here comes that dreamer." This was not a term of endearment or eager expectation. Joseph had angered his brothers with his arrogant, prideful attitude. He boastfully told them his dream that one day they would serve him. When they did not seem to get it the first time, he had another dream and told them again! Even his father, who loved Joseph the most, rebuked him for the impertinence of these dreams (Genesis 37:5–11). His dreams were so outlandish, and his announcement of them so premature, that no one could take him seriously. This kind of impractical dreaming that drives others away is not the goal of the contentment-dreaming paradox.

A few years later, Joseph should have been a poster boy for discontent. He had been sold into slavery by his brothers, but he overcame this and rose to a position of leadership and responsibility in Potiphar's house. Then he was wrongly accused of rape, framed for the crime, and thrown into prison (Genesis 37:12–36, 39:1–20). If ever someone should have given up on life, it was Joseph. His imprisonment in Egypt was the second time that he had hit bottom in life, but this was even more unfair and undeserved than the first. It would have been easy for him to decide God had abandoned him and that he was never going to realize his dreams. If we are honest with ourselves, we would admit that we want to see Joseph responding to this injustice with great fury. We would like to see him vent his anger and frustration. If not that, we would at least like to see more of the emotional struggle Joseph must have gone through as he sat in the dungeon.

Even though the Scriptures do not tell us all we might like to know, Joseph teaches us the essence of the contentment-dreaming paradox in his prison experience: "But while Joseph was there in the prison the Lord was with him; he showed him kindness and granted him favor in the eyes of the prison warden. So the warden put Joseph in charge of all those held in the prison, and he was made responsible for all that was done there. The warden paid no attention to anything under Joseph's care, because the Lord was with Joseph and gave him success in whatever he did" (Genesis 39:20–23).

How can we explain this? Our assertion is that Joseph had to be content, at some level, to excel in the ways described in this verse. This is not a "glad to be here" contentment that is based on circumstances. Rather, it is steely determination to make the best of the situation in which he found himself. Had Joseph given up, he would not have enjoyed success in whatever he did. Had he been downcast or displayed a surly attitude, the warden would not have turned to him. The verse says that God showed Joseph favor, but God's favor does not force us to act against our will. God will not force success on us. Contentment is a choice—to rely on God, and to excel no matter what the circumstances.

This does not mean Joseph was happy to be in prison. When he later interpreted the cupbearer's dream and accurately predicted the man's release and restoration, Joseph asked for a hope of deliverance (Genesis 40:1–13). He told the cupbearer, "When all goes well with you, remember me and show me kindness; mention me to Pharaoh and get me out of this prison" (Genesis 40:14). Clearly he hoped for better circumstances, but he was able to serve with excellence while waiting. Joseph did not say, "I'll start giving my best once I start getting fair treatment."

Joseph's moment of release, two years later, shows another important aspect of the contentment-dreaming paradox for second chair leaders. Finally released from prison, he found his dreams coming to fulfillment through the dreams of his first chair leader. Joseph was made the number-two person in all of Egypt because he correctly interpreted the dreams of Pharaoh, the ruler of the land. As Joseph helped to understand, implement, and achieve Pharaoh's dream, his own dream was realized as well. The dreaming side of this paradox does not minimize the dreams of those in the second chair, but it must begin with the dreams of the first chair leader. If Joseph had said to Pharaoh, "That's your dream. Now let me tell you about mine," the end of the story would have been quite different. An ongoing challenge for the second chair is finding a way to mesh your dreams with those of your first chair.

Each second chair leader with whom we spoke had an individual approach and varied stories of dealing with contentment-dreaming. All recognized the tension between the two ends of the continuum and the importance of finding the genius of the *and* in this paradox. Some, because of their circumstances and temperament, found contentment more easily than others. Some struggled with it because of the lofty dreams God put in their hearts. Some had a season when the realization of their dreams brought great satisfaction.

Peter Senge's concept of creative tension is a powerful tool for understanding and living with this paradox. In *The Fifth Discipline*, he says: "We are acutely aware of the gaps between our vision and reality. . . . These gaps can make a vision seem unrealistic or fanciful. They can discourage us or make us feel hopeless. But the gap between vision and current reality is also a source of energy. If there was no gap, there would be no need for any action to move toward the vision. Indeed, the gap is *the* source of creative energy. We call this gap *creative tension*" (1990, p. 150).

Senge continues by describing how some people begin to compromise their vision when they are faced with this creative tension. Others try to make themselves and their peers believe a picture that is not based on current reality. The challenge is to not follow either pathway to escape tension.

Second chair leaders need to learn to practice a Joseph-like contentment and at the same time never lose sight of their dreams. If God's call in your life is clear and strong, you will find yourself constantly balancing the contentment-dreaming paradox. Those who master this creative tension find a focus and energy that propels them forward in whatever way God is leading them.

8

CONTENTMENT IN
THE SECOND CHAIR

contentment
complacency

THE CONTENTMENT-DREAMING PARADOX captures the internal struggle we all encounter as leaders. This tension stems from our own understanding of our dreams and calling. You may sense that God is preparing you for a first chair role, or it may seem that you will spend your career in the second chair. Either way, you will have seasons of internal struggle, when your heart's desire seems incompatible with serving faithfully and diligently wherever God has currently placed you. But if you strive to find contentment today, God can begin to teach you to become all that you dream of being tomorrow. This does not mean you are to be so content that you become complacent. Contentment requires a long-term view that grows out of a strong spiritual foundation and continuous pursuit of God's vision for yourself and your organization. Contentment is a choice for every second chair leader.

The shape of contentment differs with the personality of the second chair leader and the context in which he or she serves. We can illustrate this with two images. When Dian Kidd and her husband, Bob, graduated from seminary, they moved to Houston so he could take a position as a chaplain in one of the city's largest hospitals. She was less clear about her career direction and ended up in an administrative position at UBA. She was clearly overqualified for the job, but opportunities for a woman in the Southern Baptist denomination are somewhat limited and she quickly fell in love with the people and the vision of the organization. Dian is particularly adept at integrating deep-and-wide thinking, so it was not long before she was promoted. Three years after her arrival, UBA adopted the concept of a "director team," and Dian was named one of the four members of this group. Talking about contentment-dreaming, she makes it clear that her dreams do not involve a future first chair assignment. She stresses that her contentment is high: "I'm a woman in Southern Baptist life, in a second chair role in the largest association in the country." Dian is a person for whom contentment comes easily because of the alignment between her dreams and her current reality.

Contentment is not so easy for Ric Hodgin, whose role as managing director of the A.D. Players makes him the second chair in this organization. Ric has been in this role for five years, and with the organization for twenty-four. His life is deeply invested in the Players, which is one of the leading Christian theater groups in the country. The A.D. Players recently completed a major property purchase that will allow construction of a dream facility. Looking from the outside, one would say Ric and Dian's situations seem similar. Both are long-term members and established second chairs in organizations that are among the best in the country in their respective arenas. But a variety of factors can steal Ric's contentment if he lets them. Questions of role definition, the demands of dealing with temperamental artists, and a heavy workload are all stresses with which he must contend. Furthermore, the opportunity to build the new theater facility creates new financial challenges and forces the Players to do planning unlike anything they have done before. Despite these challenges, Ric expresses a strong commitment to the organization, and to his first chair leader. He says he periodically has to step back and take a good look at himself and his surroundings: "When I take an honest look at my situation, I have to say I'm very blessed." Ric and Dian are just two of many expressions of contentment in the second chair.

A Picture of Contentment

"A picture of contentment" may bring to mind images of a sleeping baby or a smiling, carefree cherub. But this is not our picture of second chair contentment. We believe a mountain-climbing image is more appropriate. The peak represents your dreams and God-given potential to reach them, whether it involves moving to the first chair someday and realizing your potential there or seeing a God-sized vision accomplished as you serve in the second chair. Whatever your dreams may be, you are probably a long way from accomplishing them. The mountain-climbing analogy has several important applications for the second chair leader. Some of the world's tallest peaks are obscured by clouds for many days each year, but despite this climbers know of the summit's existence, the general direction for getting there, and how far they are from reaching it. Your ultimate dreams may not be crystal clear, but God has placed something in your heart that drives you upward and that challenges your contentment.

Mountain climbers also know that the path appearing to be shortest is not always the best or safest route. They know the ascent takes time and planning. In fact, they establish a camp at a midway point in the climb as a place to store supplies, refresh, and prepare for the final assault on the summit. Too many second chair leaders hop from one path to another. They think they can run to the top rather than taking one step at a time. They take any shortcut they find, and they certainly see no value in stopping at a midpoint camp to learn and prepare for the future.

This past summer, I (Roger) did another kind of mountain climbing while spending a few days with my family in the west Texas town of Alpine. One day we decided to hike to the sixty-five-hundred-foot peak of one of the nearby desert mountains. During the climb, I had to exercise the discipline of contentment. Just like a second chair leader, I did not have the freedom to blaze my own trail. If I had, I would have neglected the needs of my wife or father-in-law, missed out on a few great family photos, and probably gotten lost or bitten by a snake. Instead I chose to be content in bringing up the rear, holding a few barbed wire fences, and using my walking stick to check for rattlesnakes under rocks. At one point, I was no longer content to follow. I saw an opportunity to take a shorter but more strenuous path. After I left the rest of the group and committed myself, I realized I had made a foolish decision. I was on the face of a rock at a sixty-degree incline and realized I would fall thirty feet to rocks below if I slipped. I resorted to handholds, footholds, and a great deal of prayer to make it safely to the top. I had stopped choosing contentment; as a result, I found myself alone and in a dangerous spot.

All too often, second chairs lose sight of contentment in their ministry. They do not like the routes that are slower or more tedious than expected, and they certainly do not like to backtrack. Being a second chair leader always involves times when things do not move fast enough and your patience is tested. You may believe you know a better way to accomplish your dreams. Just like Roger's foolish mistake, you leave the path that the Lord has charted and go it alone, only to find yourself in a dangerous spot. Being a second chair leader brings plenty of adventure; you do not need to create it on your own.

We can return to the higher mountain peaks for one more lesson. Mountain climbing is not a sport for those seeking comfort. Snow, wind, ice, and danger are the realities of the climb. Even the midpoint camp is not a place of comfort. Though the summit is a place of victory, the conditions on top are so treacherous that the climbers stay at the summit for only a short time. Is comfort part of your definition of contentment? For climbers, contentment is not found in comfort. It is in making progress toward the summit. If you equate contentment with comfort, we hope to reshape your understanding of this paradox.

Defining Contentment

Contentment in the second chair is your choice to stay and grow and excel, for a season, regardless of current circumstances. The foremost part of this definition is that contentment is a *choice*. As we showed earlier, Joseph consistently made the choice to be content, whatever the circumstances. He excelled in slavery, in prison, and in Pharaoh's service because he chose to make the most of his time and energy. No matter the situation, position, or responsibility, Joseph chose contentment and made the most of every situation in which he found himself. Contentment is possible if you choose to understand that something more is always at work in your experiences, beyond your needs, expectations, and frustrations.

Contentment in the second chair is *your* choice. You may respond, "Of course it's my choice! What other kind of choice is there?" Too often a second chair leader allows circumstances to determine his attitude, or lets habits decide his actions, or goes along with the flow and lets other people dictate his direction. Contentment is a proactive, intentional choice. Decide in advance to be a part of fulfilling God's bigger picture for your life. Embrace the sanctifying work of the Holy Spirit that God has initiated within you. God is choosing the place and the means, but you must still choose how to respond.

Contentment in the second chair is your choice *to stay and grow and excel*. These three verbs show how second chair leaders put their choices into action. To quote John Maxwell, "God would rather place us in the crock-pot instead of the microwave" (Maxwell, 1998a). Do you feel you are in the Crock-Pot of sanctification in your second chair experience? If so, then allow the Lord to put His flavorful touches on you to further prepare and strengthen you for His service. God is in the slow-cooking process of the Crock-Pot, not the high-speed zapping of the microwave. The final quality is so much better this way. If you are constantly looking for a better offer to come along, you are not really "staying." When you choose to stay, you will not allow short-term disappointment or conflict to push you toward the exit. Staying is a commitment to remain in your current position with focus and intensity until God clearly moves you to a new place of service.

Once you decide to stay, then start growing. You will be amazed what God does if you give Him time each day. Commit to a daily time of personal growth, and be patient. Read, listen, and observe others; put the principles you are learning into action as quickly as possible. The decision to stay and grow is not a passive approach; this is why second chairs must also decide to excel. At the end of each day, have you given God the best of your time and talent? If you make the commitment to stay, grow, and excel, God can use you in powerful ways, and He can do a great work in your heart.

Contentment in the second chair is your choice to stay and grow and excel, *for a season*. This requires a big-picture understanding of your development and ministry. On the path to accomplishing your dreams, your role will eventually change. Joseph's did! Amid extreme adversity, he chose to make the most of the situation, not knowing where this attitude might take him. Ultimately, it led him to Pharaoh's court. As a believer, you can have faith that God's plans and purpose are being worked out in your life. Your role, situation, or relationship with your first chair will change with time. God will bless and honor you, even if you feel you are currently living a prison experience. After a season, He will release you from your prison or supply you with the grace and understanding you need to sustain your soul. Trust Him and He will show you great things during this season.

Contentment in the second chair is your choice to stay and grow and excel, for a season, *regardless of current circumstances*. Does this mean in every possible circumstance? No. We realize that some situations clearly call for resignation or departure. These are situations where you have given your best, but the instability of the organization or the deterioration of a relationship means it is clearly right for you to leave. "Regardless of current circumstances" is a caution against leaving prematurely at the first bump in the road. It is also recognition that unstable times and uncertain days can yield some of the greatest lessons in ministry. It has been said, "Circumstances and opportunity walk hand in hand." Who would have ever thought there would be opportunity in slavery or in prison? Yet leading through disruption and difficulty can extend your influence and sharpen your leadership. Once you realize your lack of control over circumstances, the Holy Spirit can speak God's deep truth into your life. You must be eager to see the hand of the living God at work, not only in others on your behalf but also in your life for His behalf. Paul offers a great reminder of the power of our momentary circumstances: "Continue to work out your salvation with fear and trembling, for it is God who works in you to will and to act according to his good purpose" (Philippians 2:12b-13).

Many of the second chairs we interviewed live out this definition of contentment. Kim Miller has experienced incredible growth in going from a week-by-week unpaid servant role to a vital position with widespread prominence. Warren Schuh chose to stay in periods of challenging circumstances twice when he experienced the departure of a senior pastor. The first time he guided the church through the transition and then left. The second time he led a major restructuring of the staff and stayed on board with a new senior pastor. Robin Smith sometimes was not allowed to be a leader even though he has a gift of leadership, but he refused to give up easily. Instead, he made the best of each situation until it was clear God called him to a new role. These, and many other second chairs, know that God is the ultimate source of contentment, even if it seems fleeting.

The Tension of Contentment

It is not easy to understand the timing or purpose of all that we go through. In the process of choosing contentment, we must believe God is going to show us His bigger picture some day. This is probably the thread of hope Joseph hung onto through his prison experience. It is also this hope that sustains many second chair leaders and helps them find contentment in the tension of their situation.

Guy and Kelli Caskey are an example of living for a season in the tension of contentment in the second chair. Prior to founding Crossroads Community Church in 1997, Guy was the associate pastor and youth minister at Fellowship of Champions for eight years. Kelli served with Guy in his ministry and also led a women's cell group ministry. Early in their tenure at Fellowship, Guy and Kelli began to struggle with contentment. They saw the power of cell groups and wanted to expand this ministry. They began to have a vision to reach people for Christ in nontraditional ways. But their senior pastor was slow to initiate substantial change. As a result, Guy and Kelli felt great frustration in their subordinate roles, unable to take the church to the next level and confined by the limits imposed by their first chair.

You might say, "Why didn't they leave right away? Shouldn't they have just stepped out in faith, done what they felt called to do, and left that ministry behind?" The answers are not always this clear and succinct. If you are frustrated with your first chair, it is often easier to leave than it is to stay, but the easiest path is not necessarily the best one. You may exercise more faith by staying and growing for a season than by leaving. Ask yourself, "Can I stay where I am and achieve more growth and development, both for myself and the Kingdom? Or is it better for me to leave and serve elsewhere?" For Guy and Kelli, it was both. First, it was a choice to stay and grow despite frustration, because they felt this was

God's will for a season. They believed God would honor their commitment and fulfill the dreams He had given them. When they eventually planted Crossroads, they felt a great sense of God's confirmation and blessing for their decision to have stayed for a time.

Second chairs must often discover how to choose contentment amid great frustration. You may feel you are going through a prison experience. You pray and long for freedom, yet God does not release you from this setting. In such times, you may feel loss, hopelessness, fatigue, restlessness. Your emotion is screaming at you to leave and find rest and relief, but you know in your heart that you are right where God wants you.

Once again, the choice is yours. You must decide how to handle this frustration and discontent. Can you find contentment in a season of frustration? More than that, can you learn from this season so that ultimately you are better equipped and able to handle all that God has in store for you? Are you willing to stay and grow and excel, regardless of current circumstances, if it helps you accomplish your dreams? This is a crucial decision that determines the long-term success of many second chairs.

Guy and Kelli are great examples of second chair leaders who chose the path of growth and development. Frustrated with their first chair, they made the mature choice to serve their senior pastor, even though they did not see eye to eye. Kelli concludes, "The greatest thing we could do was to make him great." This is conduct that God honors, and it is a model for all second chairs. We see it in Joseph's life, and we see it in maturing, growing second chair leaders. If you do not feel you can honor your first chair, then ask yourself whether or not you are choosing contentment and doing your ministry as unto the Lord. Guy and Kelli know their experience in the second chair helped them become better leaders. They are more sensitive to people's needs, especially those of the second chair leaders who now serve with them. The lessons in the second chair differ for each of us, but the principle of learning in the tension of contentment is applicable to all. Learn from your second chair experiences and apply them to your current and future ministry. As this happens, your colleagues, congregation, and first chair will all see you developing the potential that God has given you, and your ability to influence the organization will grow exponentially.

Waiting in the Second Chair

Some second chair leaders see their current role as a destination. They are like Kim Miller, who loves her role because she has "every opportunity to live out my gifts and calling." They still have frustrations and stresses, but most days they thank God the lines have fallen in pleasant places in their ministry (Psalm 16:6). Other second chairs would describe their current place of service as an intermediate point in the career journey. It may be a stop that is fulfilling or long-lasting, but it is definitely not the destination of their dreams. As we saw with Guy and Kelli Caskey, for some second chairs the sense of waiting can be a great challenge to contentment.

Psalm 37 is a special text for this season of waiting. It seems written just for second chairs who are struggling with the contentment-dreaming paradox. The first nine verses (particularly three through seven) are profound in their description of waiting on God: "Trust in the Lord and do good; dwell in the land and enjoy safe pasture. Delight yourself in the Lord and He will give you the desires of your heart. Commit your way to the Lord; trust in Him and He will do this: He will make your righteousness shine like the dawn, the justice of your cause like the noonday sun. Be still before the Lord and wait patiently for Him" (Psalm 37:3–7).

God has an important part in the waiting process, and so do we. These parts go hand-in-hand. Our responsibility is to trust in the Lord, do good, dwell in the land, enjoy safe pasture (or cultivate faithfulness, as in the *New American Standard*), delight in the Lord, commit our way to the Lord, trust in Him, be still before the Lord, and wait patiently for Him.

In a season of waiting, we have a lot to do! We are responsible to trust in Him and do good at every opportunity. In doing this, we can cultivate faithfulness wherever He has placed us. As we worship God, we are to commit our lives and ways to Him. These responsibilities are great reminders of how we should be living in faith if we truly trust God in our season of waiting on Him.

It appears that Joseph did exactly these things during his seasons of waiting. He believed God was ahead of him, working things out for His bigger, unseen purposes. Joseph chose to make the best of each situation, so he cultivated faithfulness everywhere he went. The Scripture shows that God was with Joseph, and we see that Joseph honored God with his actions, displaying his commitment and trust in the Lord.

It is easy to see our responsibility in this passage, but do we see the good part—God's part? Do we see God's response to our responsibility? Psalm 37:4 and 6 promise that God will give us the desires of our heart, make our righteousness shine like the dawn, and make the justice of our cause like the noonday sun.

Do we need to say anymore about God's response in our seasons of waiting on Him? No matter how hard we try, manipulate, or jockey for position, we can never capture the desires of our heart or make the justice of our cause shine like the noonday sun. Simply stated, there are great advantages in choosing contentment and waiting on God. He will do what we cannot do, even in our greatest strength and effort. We are responsible for the waiting, trusting, and dwelling. He is responsible for the outcome.

Robert Moore, who is now the senior pastor of Christ the King Lutheran, experienced a season of waiting and trusting. When he accepted the call as associate pastor at Christ the King in 1993, he viewed the position as an opportunity to learn, grow, and prepare himself for an eventual senior pastor's role. In his denomination, an associate cannot be elevated to the senior role in the same church without a special exception from the bishop. Robert was determined to serve his senior pastor and the congregation faithfully, and to trust God with the rest. Four years later, he began to explore opportunities outside of Christ the King and was actually offered a dream position to start a theological institute in Wittenberg, Germany. It was then that the president of the church council and the bishop both counseled him to stay because he was being groomed to replace the senior pastor, who was nearing retirement. Because of the denominational norms, Robert had neither sought the position nor considered this to be a plausible outcome. He still had to wait another year and deal with some difficult transition issues, but God blessed Robert's faithfulness and patience in this season of waiting.

We all go through seasons of waiting, whether in a prison experience or something less drastic. Even if we are not waiting for God to move us somewhere else, we may have to wait for an organization that does not change quickly enough. How we respond while waiting tells us (and those around us) much about our faith. Two competing forces pull at us during these seasons: the pace of society and the grace of God.

The pace of society tells us we should always be on the lookout for the next opportunity, never staying in one place too long. Some in vocational ministry keep an ear to the ground for a plum position and then seek to get their name in front of the committee, the influential gatekeeper, or the bishop. They may give little thought to the unfinished work where they currently serve. In fact, those who remain in one place for an extended period and tell others they are waiting on God may be ridiculed. Someone is sure to respond, "God helps those who help themselves." This may be a mantra for our society broadly, but it is not a verse in the Bible.

The cruelest part of the clash between society's pace and a season of waiting is the false hope that is often created. A second chair in a difficult setting may eventually find contentment, and then the hint of a way out sets his head spinning. He can think of nothing other than the joy of escape and the unfair drudgery and stress of his current role. Then, more often than not, the opportunity fails to materialize and he is left to struggle with contentment again. This is implied in Joseph's story. After interpreting the cupbearer's dream, Joseph requested, "But when all goes well with you, remember me and show me kindness, mention me to Pharaoh and get me out of this prison" (Genesis 40:14). Knowing that the cupbearer was about to be restored to Pharaoh, Joseph saw his big opportunity to get his name before the king and be released from prison. But as the days and weeks passed, Joseph's request must have resulted in only more frustration. He must have believed the cupbearer would come through for him. Joseph clearly had a special talent that could help Pharaoh; besides, the cupbearer owed him a favor. Just like Joseph, when we succumb to a pace imposed by others we often expend a lot of energy, only to end up back where we started but with our emotional and spiritual tank on empty.

Thankfully, God's grace seeks to offset and overcome our impatience. In the challenging seasons of waiting, we have a unique opportunity to experience the grace of God at a whole new level. He pours His grace over each of us in the kindness that we experience inwardly and the favor with others that we experience outwardly. God does this differently with each person. We do not know how He extended His grace to Joseph, but Scripture bears ample testimony of its power in Joseph's life. You might feel overwhelmed by your present circumstances. You feel you could abandon it all—your ministry, your faith, your church family, everything! You do not understand why you are in this prison experience or what you did to deserve it. Especially at this point, cling to the kindness and favor of God as a means to move ahead, one day at a time. Robin Smith, who has endured some difficult seasons of waiting, says he has often prayed, "God, I am asking today for the ability to cast all my cares on You." As you walk through a season of waiting in tension, frustration, and heartache—and ultimately contentment—may God strengthen you by His grace!

Sources of Contentment

How can we experience God's grace as we seek to find contentment in the second chair? What specific steps should we take? There is no simple formula, but it is helpful to keep some sources of contentment in mind. Kevin Lawson writes, "It is important to know yourself, how God has gifted and called you. This kind of knowledge can help associate staff members find contentment in ministry"(2000, p. 13). Lawson's *How to Thrive in Associate Staff Ministry* describes several sources of contentment that second chair leaders should understand and develop.

Your identity in Christ should be your greatest source of contentment. Greg Hawkins considers this to be foundational for any second chair leader: "I'm subordinating myself to God in this role. If I feel tension between a dream and my position, I have to trust God will resolve it." If our relationship with our Father is right, then we can keep everything else in proper perspective. Kelli Caskey's philosophy of ministry is to "do well what we believe God wants us to do, and the rest will come." As she reflected on the challenges she faces, she talked about the importance of "being confident in who God made me to be."

Lawson dedicates an entire chapter to help associate staff members understand their need for spiritual growth: "Of all the advice on how to thrive offered by veteran associate staff members in this study to those just beginning, the most frequently mentioned was taking time to nurture and maintain personal spiritual vitality" (2000, p. 72). Being in a ministry leadership role, whether first or second or any other chair, does not guarantee spiritual depth. In fact, the very demands of ministry can squeeze the spiritual vitality out of the leader's life. Regardless of where you serve, allow time for the Spirit to sustain and strengthen your soul. If your daily walk is not rooted in Christ, contentment will always escape you.

Another source of contentment is calling. Do you remember your calling? What process did God take you through to help you discover your calling? How has your calling grown over time? Reflecting on these important questions can keep you anchored amid great frustration and discontent. As you seek to thrive in the second chair, your calling will always be at the heart of your contentment. Lawson references H. Richard Niebuhr, who described the aspects of calling to vocational ministry. One is the "secret call," which Lawson defines as "an inner urgency to serve God vocationally. Most thriving associate staff members report that they have a clear sense of calling from God to serve in an associate staff ministry. For some this 'secret call' is a general call to serve the church; for others it is focused on a particular area of ministry, such as children's ministry or leadership of music and worship" (p. 11).

Lawson's research focused on individuals who have spent their career in associate staff roles, but we recognize that some are not called to the second chair as their career destination. Mike's calling is to the second chair, while Roger's is ultimately to the first chair. In the growth of Roger's calling, however, he has sensed a specific call to serve our senior pastor and our church. At times in his ministry, his calling was all he had to hang onto. In a season of this sort, there are countless benefits from reflecting on your own calling. To summarize Lawson, understanding your calling brings peace of mind for your ministry. It helps you persevere, discover your passion, and provide you with joy and fulfillment, especially in difficult seasons of ministry (pp. 13–16): "A strong and clear call can help an associate staff member face those pressures and that spirit of discontent and find real satisfaction in her ministry in the present, instead of anxiously looking forward to some change in the future" (p. 16).

Contentment can also be developed and encouraged through relationships, both inside and outside the church setting. In a recent conversation, Roger encouraged a young pastor to cultivate relationships outside the church in order to give himself a break from ministry. This young man is single, lives near his church, and is totally dedicated and committed to teenagers and their spiritual growth and success. He found himself discouraged, discontent, and wondering about his impact in the lives of his teens. More than anything, he described himself as "weary, wondering whether I am doing any good at all."

This relational challenge may be particularly acute for vocational second chair leaders. They frequently find their position makes it difficult to develop deep relationships with others in the congregation, but their schedules leave little time for outside relationships. Greg Hawkins described it as loneliness in the second chair. Warren Schuh is intentional in "associating with like-minded people" outside his church. Regardless of how this issue is addressed, we all need balance in our lives. The opportunities for ministry are always greater than the time available, so we must prioritize our activities and pace ourselves for the long run. It is essential for second chair leaders to nurture healthy, vibrant, life-giving relationships that help them find rest and strength for the ministry seasons that lie ahead.

The fruit of the ministry is a final source of contentment. Geoff Surratt said, "Contentment comes in trying to celebrate where we are occasionally, but then we immediately move to what's next." This captures the reality for many second chair leaders in dynamic organizations. Geoff acknowledged that contentment does not come easily because he is always dreaming of more and better things that he and his church can do.

What kind of results, in organizational and personal terms, are occurring on your watch? Results such as congregational growth, a surge in baptisms, and increasing receipts can encourage second chair leaders in their ministry. You already know, however, that the real fruit is not in quantitative measures but in changed lives. In one very difficult season at Crossroads Community Church, a small group disagreed vehemently with a decision Guy and Kelli Caskey had made. These vocal people chose to leave the church and tried to take others with them. One thing that sustained Guy and Kelli was pointing to the fruit of their labor, those who had accepted Christ through the ministry of Crossroads. Kelli remembers saying, "We owe it to those who are left to 'get back on the horse.'"

Lawson offers one specific tactic in this vein, called "savoring ministry joys": "Since some of the joys of ministry can be fleeting experiences, thriving associate staff members have found ways to 'capture the moment'. . . . Many associate staff members have put together a file or box where they place thank-you notes, letters of encouragement, and other mementos of ministry highlights. When they begin to grow tired or discouraged in ministry, they open up that file or box and read through the contents, taking time to remember how God has worked in the past" (2000, p. 134).

Identity in Christ, calling, life-giving relationships, and the fruit of ministry are all important sources of contentment. Which one do you most need to develop at this point in your second chair journey?

Challenges to Contentment

Contentment is a powerful, God-given force that allows you to thrive in your current setting. But far too often contentment is lost when a second chair falls victim to personal shortcomings. Contentment is not guaranteed. Even when a situation seems ideal, forces are working to change the dynamic and drain your contentment. Some of the forces are completely beyond your control. You might have an incredible relationship with your first chair, and then she resigns and moves to another organization. Or a sudden turn in the ministry's financial picture forces you to shelve a much-anticipated new program. Other forces that steal contentment are more within your control. Three of them are *lack of patience* with God's timing, *lack of awareness* of God's bigger picture, and *lack of skills* to do the work that is required.

The most obvious of these is lack of patience. We have already discussed how you, as a second chair leader, must be willing to wait your turn and go through God's development process. If you lack patience, you will take apparent shortcuts that in the end hinder your progress. Patience is a choice. You can choose to be content when your first chair makes a decision that creates frustration and discomfort for you. You can celebrate the ministry's accomplishments even though it seems progress is slow. Impatience easily leads to insistence on getting your way according to your timing. This is a formula for failure because it leads to loss of respect from your first chair. If you insist on doing it your way, it may be better for you to leave and do it somewhere else. Second chair leaders need to discover God's heart for them in these critical roles, and not act on their impatience by leaving too soon or trying to force their ideas to be adopted. Recognize the organizational and relational damage that can be caused by a lack of patience, and ask God to give you His long-term perspective.

Impatience can be fueled by lack of awareness of God's plans at work in our lives and our ministries. We fall prey to this ignorance when we think that leaving our current ministry situation will solve all of the problems we are having in the second chair. We tend to think that the grass is greener anywhere other than where we are, when the truth of the matter may be quite different. We often show lack of awareness by making broad-brush statements about the right preaching method, music style, or ways to reach people. This often happens when we are frustrated with an out-of-date approach in our church that we think is no longer culturally relevant. Or we think we know the best solution to a complex problem and are upset when the first chair does not heed our counsel.

Many second chairs are unaware of the complexity and pressure of the first chair's job. Any statement that begins, "If I were in the top role, I would . . ." probably is based on the second chair's lack of knowledge. In any setting (but especially in a church), the leadership challenges are incredibly complex. Scott Rambo, now the senior pastor of The Bridge Fellowship of Sugarland (Texas), reflected on how his perspective changed after moving from a second chair role into his current position: "There is so much more at stake when leading as the senior pastor than there ever was leading as the associate pastor." Second chair leaders who are sure they know all the mistakes being made by their first chair are likely to be ignorant or insubordinate. Many younger second chairs are unconscious of their need to grow and develop in their leadership abilities. Lack of awareness of one's own ignorance is a real barrier to contentment. Ignorance may be bliss, but it does not make for effective second chair leaders. Each step along the way, God desires to be at work, in and through you, to accomplish His purposes. If you are unaware of this fact, you will find it difficult to walk in a season of contentment.

Lack of skills to accomplish the requirements of your job will surely challenge contentment. If your performance is mediocre, it also undermines the contentment of your first chair and other team members! This inability may relate to performing specific tasks. A typical second chair job has a variety of requirements, and many of the people in the role lack the training to prepare them for this breadth of responsibility. Staff management may be difficult if you have always been a solo performer. Financial administration may cause you great stress if you are not adept with numbers. If you know your skills do not match the position, it is hard to be content.

The ability gap may relate less to specific skills and more to the second chair's overall productivity and responsiveness to changing circumstances. A new, young member of the children's staff at West University Baptist was curious and frustrated that others did not seem to have time to drop what they were doing and chat when he came by their office to visit. As this behavior continued, Roger confronted him and said it appeared he was more interested in making friends than doing his ministry and growing through its challenges. It felt as though we were all racing down the highway at seventy miles per hour as he would pull into the flow of traffic going thirty-five. Fortunately, the young man got the message and began to make contributions to the team.

As ministry accelerates, inability to raise your level of output is costly. Remember, leading from the second chair requires that you influence the entire organization. If your inability to meet a growing challenge threatens your place on the team, recognize the problem and seek help from a mentor. Otherwise, you will tend to shrink back, try to cover your shortcomings, and watch the more capable second chair leaders pass you by.

In *Good to Great,* Jim Collins captures the heart of contentment as we define it. He contends that organizations (and leaders) that truly excel "retain faith that you will prevail in the end, regardless of the difficulties *and* at the same time confront the most brutal facts of your current reality, whatever they might be" (Collins, 2001, p. 86). He calls this the Stockdale Paradox, named after Adm. Jim Stockdale, the highest-ranking U.S. military officer in the "Hanoi Hilton" prisoner-of-war camp in Vietnam. Stockdale used this principle to sustain his spirit in a morale-crushing prison experience. He never lost hope that he would eventually be released, but he guarded against the false hope that his freedom was imminent. Second chair leaders must have faith that God has a plan for their lives and that He knows all their needs. They have to believe that God will work in and through them, even in the most challenging situations. Whatever your current circumstances may be, our hope is that you choose to find contentment as you stay and grow and excel in the second chair.

9

DREAMING IN THE SECOND CHAIR

WHAT ARE YOUR DREAMS? In your heart of hearts, what do you long to see God do in and through your life? How has God challenged you to reach your fullest potential to accomplish those dreams? These questions lie at the heart of your leadership journey. They drive your sense of destiny and purpose in life.

Vocational second chair leaders often think they are not allowed to dream big dreams. We have a sense of purpose found in our calling, but unfortunately it stops there. We never take the next step of contemplating where this might lead. We graduate from seminary and go to our first church, with our mind full of lofty goals. As we begin to pursue our ideals, frustration sets in because no one seems to be listening and changes are taking too long. Instead of continuing to dream big dreams, we walk away with our head hung low because too many hurdles are in the way. Eventually, we stop challenging the process. We adjust and acclimate to a new reality, one that does not frustrate us because it does not involve any of our dreams. We grow numb with doubt or uncertainty and wait for a neon sign to point us in the right direction.

Whether you are vocational or volunteer, this chapter is written to encourage you to remember and pursue your dreams. In the previous chapter, we talked about finding contentment in the second chair as you grow and develop. In this chapter, we move to the other end of the paradox and examine how to dream in this unique position. You must pursue your dreams wholeheartedly! You should be scared of *not* fulfilling your dreams. God made the human heart to dream, and the dream that is most fulfilling of all is the one He has put into your heart.

When was the last time you took a break from the rush of your every-day priorities and reflected on the dreams God has placed in your heart? We have already discussed how your calling can be a source of content-ment, but it is more than that. As your calling develops through seasons of waiting and life experiences, what ultimate purpose do you discover for your life? Has God set a unique dream or vision deep inside your heart as you pursue His purposes?

Some second chairs sense that their current role is the fulfillment of God's dreams for their lives. Kelli Caskey is passionate about reaching people for Christ through authentic worship and close-knit community. She also believes that missions should be integrated into the life of the church, not left as an awkward appendage. Kelli is privileged to serve and shape the direction of a church that mirrors these values. Ric Hodgin knows that God has gifted him as an actor and a leader. He is thankful to be a second chair in one of the country's leading Christian theaters. Bob Johnson chose to leave a senior pastor role to become an executive pas-tor because he saw it as the way to realize his desire to have the greatest possible impact for the Kingdom.

Even if their current roles are not the ultimate fulfillment of the dreams God has given them, many second chairs are confident they are moving in the right direction. Geoff Surratt says, "I'm not sure that I'm called to a second chair role forever." But he makes it clear that he experiences the joy and excitement of pursuing his dreams in his current position. Robin Smith has served less than five years in several second chair roles; in each position, God shapes Robin and reveals more of His calling to him.

What do you see as you reflect on God's calling in your life? We want to encourage you to continue dwelling on this issue in the coming days. Take a day or two and journal your ultimate dreams for your ministry. Do it for a week and ask God to show you what it will take to accom-plish those dreams. Dream cultivation plays a significant role in your lead-ership journey. If you can articulate your dream, how will you begin to fulfill it? Begin to lay out the road map ahead, clearly stating as best you can the steps for accomplishing this God-given dream. You will not know all of them, but you should be able to see far enough down the road to get started. These steps act as road signs along the way to measure progress toward your destination.

We are not trying to present a complete look at the process of hearing God and discerning a personal vision. Resources such as Andy Stanley's *Visioneering* (1999) or John Maxwell's *Your Roadmap for Success* (2002) are helpful for those who want a deeper look at this question. As in the other chapters of this book, our focus is on the unique issues and opportunities related to second chair leadership. In this position, you are not limited to fulfilling the dreams of your first chair leader. You are called to be loyal and supportive, but this does not negate your sense of calling. You should have your own dreams and aspirations concerning your organization, career, and family. Furthermore, you should expect to realize these dreams, even if you never leave the second chair.

Dream Stewardship

Have you ever thought of yourself as a steward of your dreams? As with any gift that God gives us, we should be good stewards of the dreams our Maker has planted in our hearts. Joseph teaches us much about dream stewardship. The lessons are both positive and negative. He was absolutely correct in his understanding of the dreams God had given him. Yet in his youth, he was a terrible steward of those dreams. He was careless with a gift from God, in the same way that many teens today are reckless with money or cars. Just as slavery and prison taught Joseph about contentment, it appears he also learned much about dream stewardship in those years. When his brothers arrived in Egypt in search of food, Joseph was gripped with the realization that God was finally fulfilling his dreams (Genesis 42–45). What are the key lessons of dream stewardship?

Be Careful What You Say and to Whom You Say It!

God may have put deep, wonderful, lasting, eternal dreams in your heart. You may long to accomplish them for His sake, but your audience may not be able to understand or appreciate them. Your senior pastor or a fellow staff member may hear your comments about your future and think you have lost your mind. Their attitude may be, "Dream on, but don't expect it to happen here." They may start viewing you as a threat and begin pulling away from you. Joseph's brothers definitely did. His announcement of his dreams earned a rebuke from his father, the jealousy and hatred of his brothers, and a one-way ticket to Egypt as a slave.

In *Visioneering,* Stanley illustrates this principle as he writes about Nehemiah's vision of rebuilding the walls of Jerusalem: "Walk before you talk; investigate before you initiate. When God first lays something on your heart for you to do, don't tell anybody. To begin with, nobody is going to be nearly as excited as you are. Their lack of zeal has the potential to shut you down before you get started. To share a vision prematurely usually guarantees a less than warm reception" (1999, p. 75).

It is difficult to sit on something that evokes joy and anticipation within you. When you catch a glimpse of what God has in store for your future, it is natural to get so excited that you share it with anyone who will listen. But Stanley is right! All too often, we share our ideas with youthful exuberance, only to have people tell us why we cannot accomplish something of that magnitude.

Does this mean dreams can never be shared? Stanley continues to unpack Nehemiah's experience by pointing out that he prayed and fasted first. After receiving the king's permission and arriving in Jerusalem, he surveyed the wall with only a few men. Only after this preparation did Nehemiah reveal his dreams to the people. In some seasons and some situations, it is premature to reveal your dreams to anyone.

You may, however, have a confidante who can be trusted with your dreams. This is probably someone outside of your organization who has a deep, long-standing relationship with you. She will know you well and has been a voice of truth in your life. She may be a spouse, but be aware that your dreams can also become a burden for her. If you are not blessed with a trusted advisor, it is best to keep your dreams to yourself until God's plans and timing are clear. Some people in your life are not prepared to bless the dreams God has put inside you. Be careful what you share, when you share, and with whom you share it!

Check Your Ego at the Door

The timing and the audience for sharing your dreams are important, but so is how you share them. Those with great dreams may also have great confidence that they will accomplish them with God's help. Sometimes the part about "with God's help" gets lost. They may be perceived as egotistical, arrogant, or overconfident. This perception may or may not be accurate, but either way it can have a significant impact on the future of your dreams. Your willingness to humbly serve others, before and after disclosing your dreams, helps ensure that you are not wrongly characterized as an arrogant dreamer.

Not following this principle is what got Joseph into trouble. Did his arrogance as he expressed his dreams make the vision any less valid? Did his haughtiness prevent the dreams from being fulfilled? The dreams were not disqualified, but the dreamer had to go through an intense refining and humbling process to prepare him for dream fulfillment.

Too many leaders, second chair or otherwise, believe having a dream gives them the right to pursue it at all costs. As they pursue, they alienate others and cause organizational havoc. They act as if God needs their help, rather than the other way around. Second chairs need to tread lightly as they first move toward a vision. We were impressed as we saw the patience and humility of the second chair leaders we interviewed. They did not doubt their calling or dreams, but neither did they insist on having it *now*. Many waited longer than they expected to take the next step in their career. One relinquished some of his official authority in order to build a relationship with a subordinate staff member. These are not the actions of someone with a me-first attitude. They are the attitudes and behaviors of a leader who trusts God as he dreams.

God is responsible for putting the dream in your heart; you are the steward once the dream is planted. Joseph's poor initial stewardship resulted in struggle and turmoil for years to follow. The bigger the dream God has given you, the more humble you should be about it. Be a good steward with whatever He entrusts to you. Leave your ego behind; it is God's dream.

Practice Both Now and Later

Dream stewardship is a process. Second chair leaders must grow in their stewardship of all that God puts before them. The lesson of "both now and later" is quite simple. God expects your best effort *now* so you will be prepared for all that He plans to do in and through you *later*. Many young, high-potential second chair leaders do not seem to understand this principle. They have no true sense of God's leading for their future, nor an eye for the task at hand, and they definitely do not make the connection between the two. Dream cultivation requires understanding how your present responsibilities and experiences intersect with the future desires of your heart. It requires you to hunger for God and engage in some of the basic spiritual disciplines because they allow God's greater purposes to be revealed in your life.

Jesus teaches the lesson of both-now-and-later in the parable of the talents (Matthew 25:14–30), in which He shows the responsibility that we have to maximize our service for God's Kingdom. Each of three servants was given a sum of money to manage while the master was away, and each was expected to make the most of what he had. The closing lines of the master's address to the two faithful stewards captures the principle: "Well done, good and faithful servant! You have been faithful with a few things; I will put you in charge of many things. Come and share your master's happiness!" (Matthew 25:21). Second chair leaders must focus on the present and the future to truly maximize their talents for the Lord.

Arriving in Egypt, Joseph might not have understood what God had in store for the future, but he did maximize his use of the talent he had. His responsibilities in Potiphar's house and in prison required leadership, organization, and administration. These same talents—at a much higher level—were needed once he was given responsibility for the entire food collection and distribution system before and during the famine. Because Joseph was faithful with a few things, he was put in charge of many, and in the process he finally realized his dreams.

Practicing both now and later is not a passive approach. Roger recently had the opportunity to be reacquainted with a youth pastor who has been in ministry for two years. He has enormous potential as a worship leader and teacher, possesses strong interpersonal skills, and is in a great church. Despite this, Roger sensed that the pastor is just cruising along in his current role, waiting for the next job. He does not seem to understand why he is there or what impact his current role can have on his future. He has little motivation to go to seminary or extend his training in some other way. He is not taking the initiative to learn and develop his gifts under the mentoring of the senior pastor or worship pastor. Rather than both-now-and-later, this talented potential second chair leader seems to be practicing "whatever and whenever."

If you allow yourself to dream and keep the dream alive, it is easier to understand the sanctification and cultivation process through which God is leading you. It is also easier to thrive in your current situation because you desire to be used by God and grow for His greater work. Listen to Andy Stanley's insight concerning the principle of both-now-and-later:

> God is using your circumstances to prepare you to accomplish His vision for your life. Your present circumstances are part of the vision. You are not wasting your time. You are not spinning your wheels. You are not wandering in the wilderness. If you are "seeking first" His Kingdom where you are, then where you are is where He has positioned you. And He has positioned you there with a purpose in mind. . . . It may be difficult for you to make the connection at this point. But in time, it will come together. It always does [1999, p. 45].

Staying in place does not mean being stagnant. God can grow you tremendously through seasoning and waiting.

Several of the second chair leaders with whom we spoke could see God's perfect preparation in the earlier stages of their career. Steve Ahlquist, who recently left a second chair role in the banking industry, is using many of his administrative, financial, and construction management skills in his new role as executive director of ministry resources at North Coast Church. He can hardly contain his excitement over finding a ministry position that matches his skill set so perfectly and allows him to pursue his dreams. Warren Schuh, of Calvary Community Church, described how his experience in a variety of specific ministry areas helped him be a much more effective supervisor as an executive pastor. He also helped a prior congregation navigate a senior pastor transition, an experience that God used directly when Calvary's senior pastor retired. Mike's own story is one of several seemingly unrelated threads coming together to prepare him to leave a business career to become a second chair in a church and a consultant to other ministry leaders.

As these examples show, you never know all that God is preparing you for, so take every lesson seriously. Seek the advice of older, wiser leaders and have a teachable spirit in any situation. Use the *now* to develop into the man or woman that God longs for you to be, and you will realize the dream He has in store for you *later*.

Trust God in the Details

You have heard the saying, "the devil is in the details," but when it comes to dream stewardship we need to recognize that *God* is in the details. What does this mean? It means God may give a dream, but we usually do not know the details of how the dream is to be fulfilled. We may think we know, but presumption can actually lead to trouble. Should our assumptions about the journey toward our dreams not match the path on which we find ourselves, we might begin to doubt God or question the vision. Before this happens, we should ask whether we are assuming too much and failing to let God be in charge of the details.

Joseph probably thought he knew how his dreams would play out. We can imagine that he expected to spend his entire life in Canaan, and that one day his father would elevate him over his brothers to the position of family patriarch. Surely he did not know that the path of realizing his dreams would take him to Egypt. Although Joseph might have misunderstood, the dreams were no less valid; nor was God's role minimized in the process. God was in the details from the beginning; He just chose to conceal many of them at the outset.

After the frustration of his initial second chair experience, Glenn Smith was determined never to be an executive pastor again. It seemed obvious to him that he was not cut out for the role, and he certainly did not want to risk going through another season of intense discontent. But after several years as the pastor of a church plant, God called him to the position of executive pastor of Sugar Creek Baptist. This time, his experience was an eight-year season of God's blessings and success. Looking back, Glenn can see God's hand preparing him through those earlier experiences. He learned about the challenges of being in the first chair and how to be more effective in the second chair. He learned about the unique struggles of new churches and how to overcome obstacles. At Sugar Creek, God meshed Glenn's leadership abilities with his passion for church planting in ways that bore much fruit for the Kingdom.

If the details do not match your expectations, go back and reexamine your assumptions. God is still at work, but it may be in a way you would have never expected.

Dreaming with Your First Chair

Is it possible for second chair leaders to dream with their first chairs? Can two or more leaders dream big dreams and find common ground in them? We recognize that this is not easy; some would even say it is impossible. But if you want to reach God's dreams for yourself and your organization, it is essential. Kouzes and Posner say: "Visions seen only by the leader are insufficient to mobilize and energize. . . . [Leaders] breathe life into ideal and unique images of the future and get others to see how their own dreams can be realized by embracing a common vision" (2004, p. 53). This points toward the first chair's responsibility, but it also makes clear the importance of a shared vision. Even if your wiring is leading you toward an eventual first chair role of your own, you can still dream with the first chair where you currently serve. We encourage you to discover ways you can accomplish your dreams within the dreams of your first chair. If this does not seem possible, we still want to encourage you to be a committed, supportive advisor who works toward achievement of your first chair's dreams.

Meshing Your Dreams Within Those of Your First Chair

A first chair's dreams for the organization are often big and broad. They point toward an exciting future, but they may not answer all the *how* questions. This gives second chair leaders plenty of room to pursue their vision, so long as it is in line with the general direction given by the first chair. A first chair leader is often like a master artist, outlining a drawing and a color scheme and then letting a team of apprentices complete the painting. If the apprentices like the theme and the concept of the painting, they will enjoy completing the work of art.

Of course, this means the initial step is to truly understand your first chair's vision. Sometimes it is clear and carefully articulated. At other times, you must spend a great deal of time listening and clarifying to grasp the future that the first chair has in mind. The best way to test the clarity of a vision is to ask yourself, "Do I understand what I should be doing to help our organization pursue this vision? Can I explain the vision and its implications to someone else?" If you do not clearly understand the dreams of your first chair, find the time and the means for doing so.

Accomplishing *your* dreams, however, moves well beyond understanding the first chair's vision. Once you understand, you can begin to look for opportunities where your passion and gifts intersect perfectly with the first chair's vision. Many of the second chair leaders we interviewed found it possible to pursue their dreams within the structure of the organization and the boundaries of the first chair's dreams. Glenn Smith had a vision for church planting but was serving as the executive pastor in a large church. When his senior pastor, Fenton Moorhead, began to dream of reaching people who were unlikely to attend Sugar Creek, Glenn was able to develop and lead a church planting movement that resulted in thirty-six new churches being started. Mike Slaughter had a vision for reaching unchurched people through innovative approaches, and Kim Miller had a passion for using the arts in worship. Their visions meshed perfectly and resulted in explosive growth at Ginghamsburg Church. Geoff Surratt knew the vision of Seacoast Church was to reach the lost as quickly as possible, but a multisite approach had not occurred to him until it was suggested by his brother the senior pastor. It took Geoff time to embrace this new vision, but he eventually saw it as a God-inspired extension of the church's vision and an exciting step toward his personal dreams.

Bob Johnson offers an encouraging example of a second chair meshing his dreams with a first chair. Before coming to Chapelwood, Bob was the senior pastor of a midsized congregation in a rural town. It was not an easy decision to move back into a second chair position, leaving a first chair role where he was experiencing considerable success. As he says, "I don't get to be the lead dreamer here." So why did he make this move, a change that made little sense from a career-management perspective? Bob knew the great potential of Chapelwood and the role he could play in realizing more of these opportunities. He also knew the heart of Jim Jackson (the senior pastor), and he knew Jim would give him the chance to pursue his dream. There have been moments of frustration, but Bob looks at this move as the right decision.

Realizing your dreams within those of your first chair is another example of the genius of the *and*. It is a costly mistake anytime a second chair thinks she must choose between accomplishing her vision and pursuing that of her first chair. Preston Mitchell said it best: "I want to see this church be the best that it can be. I, as the second chair, still have dreams. My dreams are his [the first chair's] dreams." If first and second chairs see the same vision for the ministry, God's blessings are released in a powerful way.

Supporting Your First Chair's Vision

Even at times or in an area where you may not feel alignment between your dreams and those of your first chair, you still must play the role of supportive adviser. Proverbs 11:14 declares that "for lack of guidance a nation falls, but many advisers make victory sure." How can you be a key adviser who makes victory sure? You can advise your first chair how to implement the vision if you know how to listen, understand, and act.

As we have described, the most important kind of listening is to clearly hear your first chair's vision. This requires patience and attentiveness to what the first chair is saying, both privately and publicly. If the public message does not adequately communicate the vision, the second chair has a distinct opportunity to seek clarification in private. He or she is also in a unique position to help the first chair know what is being heard by others. The second chair may have a better read of the people than the first chair does. A good second chair leader understands how the vision affects the congregation and can sense whether the people comprehend and support the changes needed. If you have this understanding, you can serve as an important bridge since the best second chair advisors are those who not only understand the purpose of the dream but also assess how it is being communicated.

Beyond communication, second chairs support the vision by rolling up their sleeves and working toward the end result. If the ministry you lead is not aligned with the vision, this sends a strong, negative signal to the rest of the organization. If this occurs, other leaders will interpret support of the vision as optional or conclude you are not on the same page with the lead leader. Support for the vision must start in your own backyard. As you support your first chair's dream with your actions, ask what the broader organization must do to effectively reach its goals. What constraints exist that might keep this from happening? How might its effectiveness or efficiency be improved?

Second chair leaders should assist the first chair by clearly defining these organizational details, especially if the first chair is given to big, broad visions. The senior pastor often casts the vision while the second chair implements the details. The beauty of this relationship is the complementary way in which the two functions help grow the church. The senior pastor is sensing God's direction, painting the verbal pictures, and catalyzing the congregation, while the second chair is looking through the details of the facts, figures, personnel, finance, and ministry programs to ensure that the vision is actually being accomplished. Gary Ferbet says, "I would have made a great military officer. If you told me to take that hill, I would be sure we got the job done." Second chairs support their first chair's vision with a positive attitude and effective action.

We recently experienced all of these aspects of dreaming with our first chair during a challenging season at West University Baptist. For at least three years, our senior pastor challenged the staff and church to become more evangelistic and have more impact in our community. As the church continued to grow, our facilities became increasingly cramped. These two issues came to a head with the opportunity to acquire the facilities of a nearby church and shift to a multisite ministry model. We (Mike and Roger) both saw exciting possibilities in the change. In separate ways, God was speaking to both of us and planting this dream in our hearts. When the specific opportunity arose, we found ample room for our own dreams in the vision of our pastor.

But a vision for a second campus was not shared or understood by most of our members. The communication challenge was huge. Many people were more comfortable asking questions or expressing concerns to one of us than to our senior pastor. All three of us needed to listen to others, compare what we were hearing, make sure we were on the same page, and then clarify the message. Our timing for making the decision and our specific plans for the second campus were revised many times along the way. Even when the decision seemed in doubt, it was an exciting season of praying and dreaming together as a leadership team. Ultimately, this is what dreaming with your first chair should be: seeking God together and joining Him on an adventure forward in which you share the labor under the Lord's leadership.

Dreaming in Your Chair

Some of your dreams in the second chair have to be closely aligned with those of the first chair because of the organizationwide impact. In other situations, you can dream in your chair without this same level of close coordination. Some second chairs may feel hemmed in by a first chair's lack of vision. This makes dreaming with the first chair difficult at best, and it limits her or his ability to take any initiative on a far-reaching scale.

But many aspects of ministry do not require the hand-in-glove coordination that we described in the previous section. In most settings, you can do more than daydream in your chair; there are ways to act on your dreams. If the organizational vision is broad and the boundary lines defining your responsibilities are clear, this creates a space in which you can take initiative. In this case, the biggest constraint is your own determination to pursue your dreams.

In a previous congregation, Robin Smith felt shut out from dreaming with his first chair. The senior pastor wanted him to stay within his narrowly defined role as the music leader. Robin's suggestions for large-scale improvement either fell on deaf ears or were rejected outright. But he still had dreams of a greater Kingdom impact, particularly in the area of outreach and community transformation. He assembled a small team of like-minded lay leaders who began to pray with him for this kind of opportunity. He was careful to focus all of his ideas and energy within the boundaries of the music ministry so that he could avoid conflict or any appearance of insubordination with the senior pastor. Eventually, God gave this group a vision of a patriotic musical to be held in a local high school auditorium over the July 4 weekend. The first year, Robin's church produced a small, low-budget program with the pastor's lukewarm approval. The second year, another three churches joined in; and in the third year, it became a major community event with twelve churches participating and with his pastor as one of the event's leading proponents. Robin saw the realization of a God-given dream in a challenging leadership situation, without crossing the line of insubordination. It is possible to pursue exciting dreams, even if the second chair seems too confining.

Of course, this story is just one example. Second chairs may find themselves in a variety of situations as they seek to dream within their chair. Some first chairs are highly insecure or controlling. In this case, any kind of dreaming is difficult. Remember the lessons of defining and crossing the line, and do not place yourself in a position of insubordination. You may find that time and trust building gradually give you more freedom to act on your dreams. You may also prayerfully discern that your dreams are calling you to leave your current place (a subject we explore in Chapter Ten). At the other extreme, some first chairs are quite hands-off. If so, be careful not to run ahead of your first chair. Even a seemingly detached first chair should be kept informed and be able to shape the direction of the second chair's dreams.

Another aspect of dreaming in your current chair is developing the people who serve with you in your ministry area. If your influence with others adds value to the entire organization, then you should dream with the people in your ministry. As we saw in the story of Robin Smith, this dreaming must not be done in a way that opposes or threatens the first chair. As you dream with your team, you add value by helping them discover and begin to accomplish their dreams. You can also furnish resources, lend an ear to them in times of trouble or discord, or send them for training. As you invest in them, they will see you as a trusted partner and you will have more opportunity to hear and encourage their dreams. You might say, "What is your dream for the student ministry?" As they express it, you have an opportunity to affirm and coach them. If you fail to do so, their capacity to grow and reach their God-given potential may be stifled. If you make the investment, you can help them accomplish their dreams by showing them the way, making the necessary tools available, and speaking vision into their lives.

Dreaming in your chair requires two other attributes: effective communication and realistic expectations. In our discussion of dreaming with your first chair, we highlighted the importance of communication for clarifying the vision. Another kind of communication is needed if you are going to dream in your chair. Your first chair has to know something about your dreams. He or she might give you more freedom to pursue this calling if you take the risk to reveal it. At the same time, your expectations should be realistic. If you are a new associate pastor, do not tell the senior pastor you hope to take over within two years! Do not even say that you expect to share equally in the leadership and preaching, unless this was explicitly discussed in advance. Be patient with the process, and realize that the path to seeing dreams fulfilled is never quick or easy.

Dreaming in your chair is no less valuable than dreaming with your first chair. Both should ultimately be guided by God and give glory back to Him. When you get down to the details, whether dreaming in your chair or dreaming with your first chair, you should always have a Kingdom perspective. It should guide everything you do: the tough decisions on personnel, management of limited resources, the choice among attractive ministry options. As long as God is the source and the focus of your dreams, you are on the right path.

Dreaming Beyond Your Chair

Does your dreaming lead you to envision an influence beyond your chair, beyond the four walls of your church or the mission of your organization? God may have given you a dream for a broader Kingdom impact. If so, you do not necessarily have to choose between your current second chair role and this external dream. Glenn Smith was still the executive pastor at Sugar Creek when he established New Church Initiatives (NCI), an organization that trains church planters and encourages church planting movements all around the world. He eventually felt called to NCI as a full-time endeavor, but his story is the exception. More often, second chairs see the world beyond their chair as a place to be refreshed, or a place in which to use their gifts and passions differently. Warren Schuh says that one way he finds contentment is by discovering outlets beyond his local church. We are not talking about leaving your current position; that is the subject of the next chapter. Instead, we are talking about dreams and opportunities that are outside your role and your organization but that can be attained without a change in your career or position.

Dreaming beyond your chair may take you to a place of high visibility and recognition. Most prominent Christian leaders today are known because they pursued a God-given dream to expand their influence while continuing to serve in their local churches. Leaders such as Bill Hybels, Rick Warren, Andy Stanley, Max Lucado, and Chuck Swindoll are a few of the many local church leaders who have far-reaching influence that grew out of far-reaching dreams. Others have dreams that take them beyond their chair less conspicuously. They might serve as an adjunct professor at a seminary or write Bible study curricula. They serve with inner-city or international missions organizations, or they compose music.

We are privileged to work with one such musician, Lee Poquette. Lee recently was honored when one of his arrangements was played for the president of the United States as part of a special ceremony in Washington, D.C. Lee is a genuinely humble man whose unique gifts enable him to capture our faith powerfully through music. He composes because of his love for music and for God, and then he makes his arrangements available. Though he has become well-known in his sphere, it is not necessary to claim a big name and a grand stage to accomplish Kingdom tasks. You can simply begin to dream from your current chair and ask God to give you an exponential influence.

If you make this request, you should also be prepared to pay the price. This may entail time away from family as you compose or write or earn another degree. You may experience disappointing setbacks or feelings of loneliness because no one understands your dreams. Any dream that is worth pursuing has a price. When the pieces finally fit together, Joseph understood the price of a dream that was far beyond his original chair. He realized God had been at work in a greater way than he could see, but the price was high. Joseph's recognition of God's larger plan was clear when he revealed his identity to his brothers: "And now, do not be distressed and do not be angry with yourselves for selling me here, because it was to save lives that God sent me ahead of you. . . . God sent me ahead of you to preserve for you a remnant on earth and to save your lives by a great deliverance. So then, it was not you who sent me here, but God" (Genesis 45:5, 7–8a).

The last piece of the puzzle was inserted when his family came in search of food. It is amazing how clearly Joseph understood the God aspect of his journey. In coming to this realization, he could also put the great price he had paid into perspective.

The book you hold in your hands is itself a result of dreaming beyond a chair. Much of what we have written comes from on-the-job training as we served the people of West University Baptist Church. As we learned and dreamed, we could not stop with applying the lessons in just one church body. We wanted to share it with others so they might grow stronger in their own leadership journey. Mike's path toward broader Kingdom impact began with his first book, *Leading Congregational Change,* and it has continued with a variety of consulting and speaking opportunities. Roger began praying five years ago: "Lord, if you are willing, I would like to write." We have both learned much in this process. Even as we were writing "beyond our chair," we took many of the lessons back to our chair. We paid an obvious price in the hours taken to prepare this manuscript. For Roger, an additional cost was to remain in the second chair longer than he anticipated or even wanted. But Roger now sees that if God had given him a senior pastor's chair when he wanted it, he might have missed the Kingdom opportunity to equip other leaders. Just as we have been given the privilege of dreaming beyond our chair, we hope this offering will be of value to many men and women in the second chair.

10

LEAVING THE SECOND CHAIR

HAVE YOU EVER ENTERED a living room in someone's home and chosen a particular place to sit because it looked comfortable? After sitting a few minutes, you thought to yourself, "I wish I hadn't chosen this seat. It isn't a comfortable chair for me. Maybe I should get up and move to another chair." Too many second chair leaders do the same with their careers. A seemingly attractive chair turns out to be uncomfortable, or it becomes worn and tattered. When this happens, human nature pushes us to go chair shopping, and maybe even to get a new chair. Sometimes it is exactly the right thing to do. After serving faithfully for a season, God may be calling you to move. Sometimes, however, you contribute to the problem by picking the wrong chair, or failing to see the benefits of your current position. Leaving well is rarely easy, but it is certainly important.

Roger recently spoke with a pastor who wondered if he was following God's will when he left his second chair role to take a position as a senior pastor in another state. Roger remembers small-group settings in which this pastor would ask for prayer concerning his desire to leave. When the opportunity arose, it seemed to be an answer to prayer, and he left his uncomfortable second chair. Several months later, he reflected, "I don't know if I was in God's will. I am not sure whether it was truly His plan, or whether He allowed me to do this because I was so determined to leave." This pastor's new first chair role became uncomfortable very quickly. Roger responded, "I was just reflecting on this (in preparation for this chapter). I don't want to feel as if I have to leave my second chair. I don't want to be in a situation that is so bad that I can't stay or that I can't leave well."

Almost all second chair leaders leave their position eventually, but not all leave well. One notable hindrance to the long-term success of second chair leaders is when they move prematurely or leave poorly. In doing so, they may miss valuable lessons that would serve them well. Or they may leave a trail of damaged relationships in their wake. Those who leave well are 110 percent committed until the end, keeping their focus on God and seeking the best for the ministry they serve. Some leave for a first chair role, some take a new second chair position, and others retire or simply resign. Whatever you think the future may hold, you can benefit by reflecting on the timing and the process of leaving the second chair well.

Before You Arrive . . .

The process of leaving well begins before you arrive in a second chair position. The things you ask and say, learn and clarify have a direct bearing on your future success in this role. Your success as you serve has a direct bearing on how you leave. By the same token, if you fail to prepare well you are likely to encounter problems during your tenure, which ultimately may make your departure difficult.

The burden for this advance preparation rests with you, not with your prospective first chair or organization. It begins with your decision to be honest. Far too often a candidate for a job shades the truth to fit what the potential employer wants to hear. It is better to be forthcoming about your strengths and weaknesses. You can still put your best foot forward, but you should also be prepared to answer questions about areas where you need to improve. Several things can happen if you are less than honest about your abilities and shortcomings. You may get the job and then spend the rest of your time trying to cover up for your weaknesses. Or your first chair may actually give you extra responsibilities in these areas because of your self-proclaimed strengths. This is also a time to describe some of your hopes and dreams. Disclosure is important in assessing your fit for the current role, and it is also useful for future career planning. In interviewing for a position, it is best to keep one simple philosophy in mind: if the role does not fit your *true self*, then it is not the right fit at all.

Beyond self-disclosure, it is incumbent upon you to dig deep to understand what the position entails. Too many job candidates see the interview as a one-sided affair; they answer the questions and then wait to hear if they are getting the job. You may need to wait until later in the process, after the interviewers have asked their questions, but you should have ample time to ask questions of your own. Try to learn about the first chair's personality and expectations. Ask enough questions that you can imagine what it would be like to work for her. Do her direct reports have a great deal of autonomy, or are they closely managed? Does she emphasize personal relationships with staff or is her style strictly business? What is her vision for the organization? How would she define success for your role? Pay particular attention to the first chair. If this relationship is not going to be viable, the rest of the picture is irrelevant. Similar questions should be asked of the organization in general. You may even want to talk to your predecessor in this role. When it comes to making your own assessment of a potential employer, ask questions until you cannot think of any more to ask; do not feel rushed in the process. If you are unable to envision what it will be like to serve in this position, you should probably reflect and assess further.

Bob Johnson made a thorough evaluation before accepting the executive pastor role at Chapelwood United Methodist. The move back into a second chair role was made easier because he had served previously at Chapelwood and worked for a brief time with Senior Pastor Jim Jackson. Nevertheless, Bob was careful to make sure that he understood Jim's objectives for the position and how his skills would fit. He saw a clear opportunity to complement Jim. He knew that Jim would not place unreasonable constraints on him. Even with this thorough approach, Bob says he probably did not ask enough questions about Jim's dreams. Because of his prior history, he assumed he had a clear understanding. In reality, it took him most of his first year to clearly understand the vision and its full implications. For Bob, the learning curve was steep and rewarding, but the steps he took before he arrived paved the way for a successful season in this second chair role.

"Should I Stay, or Should I Go?"

Stephen Covey teaches that we should look for win-win scenarios between parties whenever possible (1989). This is a great approach to life, but it is often difficult to achieve in leaving the second chair. If you are a high-performing leader, your church or organization may feel deep loss at your departure. If you are asked to leave, possibly during a transition of first chairs, you may feel like the loser. Even though neither seems like a win-win situation, you can work toward a mutually beneficial solution in your handling of the transition. Even if a win-win seems impossible, you can focus on the things that are in your control and trust God with the rest. So how do you know when you should stay or go?

A Matter of Timing

You may know that God is going to call you to leave, but is now the right time? Timing can be ambiguous. In one sense, there may never seem to be a right time: the church is at a critical juncture, or your kids are the wrong age for a move, or you are experiencing great results in your ministry. These are certainly factors to consider, but there is a faith factor as well. A wise minister at West University said, "When it is right for you, it is right for everyone. If the Lord is in it and He leads you away, then it will be right for everybody." This minister's name is Ronny Barner, and he served our church for thirty-six years as minister of music and administration. Ronny continued, "If it is right for me, then it will be right for the church, and God will provide the leadership the church needs in this time." When Ronny retired, it left a huge hole in our church. How would anyone fill the gap? But God had a plan that included the growth of an existing leader (Roger), a career change that brought a lay leader onto the pastoral staff (Mike), and an influx of many other talented lay leaders.

Some second chair leaders are in too much of a hurry and leave too soon. They try to force a change so they can move to the next ministry challenge, the next stepping stone in their career. As discussed in earlier chapters, choosing contentment and staying through a tough season can be a tremendous learning experience. Ask the Holy Spirit to clearly reveal if it is time for you to leave, or if you still have more to learn in your current role. If you find confusion instead of clarity, now is probably not the right time to leave. As we saw with Guy and Kelli Caskey in Chapter Eight, the decision to stay can be the right one for a leader's personal growth and in obedience to God.

You might ask, "What about my needs and those of my family as I consider whether to leave my chair?" Financial and quality-of-life factors are valid considerations as you think about your current position and the possibility of moving to another chair. One former second chair who left for a first chair position said, "No one is going to look out for your financial needs in ministry but you." Another second chair, when asked how we could pray for him, answered, "You can pray for balance in my life. This job can really take a toll on my family and me." These considerations should not be a reason for leaving your chair unless you have already tried to address them within your chair. In other words, have you taken steps on your own to gain more balance? Have you spoken to your first chair or the personnel committee chair about your financial needs? We also realize that new, outside opportunities sometimes offer significant advantages for you and your family. God has given you dreams for your family and your personal life, just as He has for your career and your ministry. If the time is right and God's hand is in it, do not be afraid to pursue those dreams.

Just as some second chairs leave too soon, others hang on too long. For their sake and for the church, they should step aside and make room for others. We have seen this happen often in student ministry. A youth pastor comes to a church full of energy and great ideas; then, for any of a variety of reasons (maturity, new spouse or children, change in calling) the ministry begins to lose momentum. Many youth pastors seem to stay at least a year too long in student ministry. They know it is time to go but are unsure how to make the transition. Youth pastors are not the only people who might stay too long in a role. If your role is not continuing to offer growth, challenge, and significant opportunities to make a difference in the organization, it may be time for a change.

Another scenario is when the organization changes in such a way that your skills no longer seem to match its needs. If you are not constantly learning and growing, you are likely to see your influence diminish. Maybe the only change you need to make is in your responsibilities, or perhaps your attitude. But if you feel stagnant for an extended time, consider the possibility of making a more radical change by leaving your chair and moving to a brand new adventure.

One reason you might stay too long is comfort with the known. The corollary is fear of the unknown. You should never become so comfortable that you are afraid to leave. If you live by this rule, you will stay fresh. If you find your groove and slip into cruise control, you will lose your leadership edge. Comfortable second chair leaders may be loved by the congregation, but neither they nor those who follow them have the energy and drive to make the ongoing changes for organizational effectiveness. Ask yourself, "What is my motivation for staying? Am I here to fulfill all that God has put in my heart, or am I just comfortable with my surroundings and enjoying the ride?" Seek contentment, but not comfort, in your second chair.

Not My Timing

What if you do not sense that it is time to leave your chair, but you are asked to exit? This is a reality for many second chair leaders. Whether it comes as a surprise or with some warning, whether it seems fair or unjust, whether it is handled well or poorly, changing chairs at the insistence of someone else is rarely easy. Of course, if it is an unfair surprise that is handled awkwardly, it can be traumatic. We said you should focus on the things within your control, so what should you do if asked to leave? Even in this difficult situation, you still control your awareness, your attitude, and your response.

The starting point is to be prepared. This does not mean you keep your resume in circulation or live with one foot out the door. You should, however, be aware of warning signs that a change may be coming. The sign may be relational stress or questions about your performance. The hints may be subtle, but you will usually have some advance indications of pending problems.

A frequent and more obvious trigger event is a change in first chair leaders. Warren Schuh correctly points out that second chair roles are the ones most at risk whenever a new senior pastor comes on board. The relationship between first and second chairs is unique; it works best when it is based on highly complementary skills and closely aligned visions. So if you have a new first chair, you may no longer be the best person for the second chair. Warren knows this from experience. He was executive pastor of Mission Hills Church in Littleton, Colorado, for ten years. When the senior pastor retired, Warren helped guide the church through the interim period, but he also knew he was not the right second chair for the new senior pastor. A few years later, he moved to his current role as executive pastor of Calvary Community Church, knowing the senior pastor was nearing retirement. The interim was a unique, and at times stressful, period of uncertainty; but Warren saw the seeds of a healthy partnership when the new senior pastor, Brad Johnson, was called to Calvary.

If a second chair is asked to leave because of a transition in the first chair, it is not an issue of competence or abilities. Greg Hawkins has been a key leader at Willow Creek Community Church for more than ten years. He knows the organization because he helped develop it, and the vision because he helped design and implement it. He also knows he might not be the right executive pastor if someone else moves into the senior pastor role. A new first chair may already have a person or a team that he works well with. Warren Schuh describes the initial transition period for an established second chair as being like "a dance, [trying] to figure out who's leading and who's stepping on toes." As you begin this dance, you may discover that your skills do not complement those of the new first chair. You could even represent a threat to the incoming leader. No one likes to talk about it, but some first chairs are insecure in their own leadership, and they cannot work well with a second chair who is well established and viewed by the organization as a vital part of the team. If you are asked to leave in this situation, remember it may not have anything to do with your performance. Remember too that God had advance warning, even if you did not. He also has a desire to conform you into His image regardless of the circumstances.

At other times, you could be asked to leave because you are perceived as lacking the necessary competence for the job. You may have done nothing blatantly wrong, such as being insubordinate, immoral, or unethical. Instead, you are perceived as not having what it takes. The apparent shortcoming may be a lack of initiative, limited influence in the congregation, or weak interpersonal skills. You may have been effective for a season, but the senior leader wonders whether you can keep up with the growing and changing requirements of the ministry. If this happens to you, what do you do? Consider asking for a second chance, for more time to prove yourself. If you are given this opportunity, work as you have never worked before. Show your team that you belong and that their perceptions were wrong.

If you have done your best—you tried to work through a transition or attempted to make the improvements that were needed—and you are still asked to leave, how should you respond? Leave well. If the issue is more personality than competence, you should ask your senior leader to help you find another place to serve. Seek advice on the type of role or organization that best fits your skills and temperament. Try to maintain positive relationships with your first chair and others on your team, even if you feel you have been treated unfairly. Do nothing that undermines them or the organization. You never know when this will come back to help or haunt you down the road. Anything negative that you say or do ultimately hurts the cause of God's Kingdom.

When Mike moved from a second chair role in business to one as a vocational staff member, it was not his first career change. He saw the win-win of God's timing on more than one occasion of leaving his chair owing to circumstances beyond his control. He had to leave companies twice during corporate takeovers, once when his division was closed, and once when he was not chosen for a key promotion. It is never easy to be told to leave, and Mike had to deal with his own feelings of rejection, inadequacy, anger, and second guessing during these times. But with each successive season of uncertainty, he learned to trust God more. He prayed, spent time with family, and enjoyed the extra time for hobbies. He did his part to find the next position, and he tried to wait on God for the rest. During one of these seasons, God provided Mike's initial opportunities to consult with churches and denominational leaders. In a second transition, Mike did much of the writing for *Leading Congregational Change*. God proved faithful in ways that Mike could never have imagined, and He will in your times of transition as well.

A Matter of Stewardship

Ultimately the decision to leave is also a decision to be a good steward of your gifts. Dena Harrison says, "Each person has a duty to God to use their gifts and not accept a situation where their gifts are not being used." If you are in a position where you consistently are stymied in using the gifts God has given you, then it is impossible for you to be a good steward. Before you resign, however, distinguish between "not fully using your gifts at this time" and "having little prospect for ever using your gifts." You may need to improve communication and exercise more patience. Perhaps you and your first chair have never had a serious discussion about your gifts and how you might use them more effectively. Perhaps your first chair is well aware of your gifts but is moving on a different timeline to develop and employ them. But perhaps the role or relationship is such that your gifts are not going to be used. If this is the case, it may be a clear sign that you should leave your chair.

The corollary to this stewardship lesson, however, is that you should not hurry to leave a position where your gifts are being used. Many second chair leaders have an artificial clock telling them when it is time to move to the next position. Their assumptions about the right way to climb the career ladder override their assessment of current ministry effectiveness. Dena Harrison's comment about using your gifts is notable because she spent five years as an assistant rector, far longer than the normal posting for this position. Even though she could have taken a call to a first chair position sooner, she chose to stay in a situation where she was able to use and continue developing her leadership gift. As a result, she was a more effective leader when she did leave. She also willingly left a first chair position to move back into a second chair role, this time at the diocesan level, because again she saw this as good stewardship of her gifts.

In a similar way, Bob Johnson chose to leave a first chair role and become a second chair leader again. He says a major difficulty in the transition has been navigating conversations with peers in his denomination who cannot understand why anyone would, as they see it, go backward in their career. Even though this has been hard, Bob is confident that God led him to this decision and that he is where God wants him to be. As you choose to be a good steward, God takes you to some unexpected and rewarding places in your career journey.

As You Go . . .

One of our deacons was recently released from his executive-level banking position in a corporate downsizing. In separate conversations, we (Mike and Roger) were both impressed with how well he was managing his career transition. His release did not seem fair, and he had his share of anger and anxiety to deal with, but he also modeled many traits that second chair leaders should practice as they go. He found appropriate ways to work through the emotions that came with the initial shock, and then he focused on the task at hand. Even as he was conducting his own job search, he was helping several valued subordinates who were also released. One notable part of his story was that many of his new job possibilities grew out of relationships that began ten to twenty years earlier. In one conversation, Roger said, Michael "do you realize that you just referenced five different relationships that are all still intact after a long period of time? I want to commend you for leaving your current situation well and also walking in right relationship with all of these colleagues over the years." Michael had not really thought about this, but he knew by intuition and experience that maintaining these positive relationships brings richness to life today and constitutes an important network for the future. Whether the departure is your choice or not, as you leave, leave well.

Prepare in Advance

Can you prepare for an unexpected loss of position and still be fully committed to serving in your current role? Most of us buy life insurance, but we do not give up on life just because we have a policy in hand. Michael's story shows one aspect of preparing in advance. Building and maintaining relationships should be an ongoing process. Do this because of your love for people and because it is the right thing to do, not because you expect to leverage these relationships in the future, and you will have a network of friends who could hold the keys to your next step in a time of transition.

Preparing in advance also has a financial dimension. The shock of an unexpected job loss is often compounded by the panic of an impending cash crisis. Vocational ministry is not a high-paying profession, and ministry leaders do not receive a golden parachute when they leave a church or judicatory. It may not be easy, but a good way to prepare for a transition is the practical habit of regularly putting a small portion of your income into a rainy-day savings account. Even a small reserve can be invaluable if you are faced with an unexpected job loss. Depending on your circumstances, you should also seek to negotiate an adequate separation package that includes several months of salary and benefits. In business, it is common to do this at the time an executive is hired. Even if it is impractical to do so in advance, second chair leaders who have given their best to the organization should have no qualms about asking for reasonable transition compensation as they leave. If a lump sum separation package is not granted, you may reach an agreement to continue working in your current role while you look for new employment. Do not be timid; it is appropriate to ask for fair financial treatment at the time of your exit.

The most important aspect of preparing in advance is mental. As we have said, the second chair is a unique role in a unique relationship with the first chair. The stories of leaders such as Ronny Barner—who stayed in his second chair role for more than three decades under three senior pastors—are the exception. Anyone who thinks she is assured of remaining in her current position is probably setting herself up for disillusionment and frustration. No one is guaranteed a long career in one place or a dream promotion or even fair treatment at the hands of the first chair. Paul's instruction was that "whatever you do, work at it with all your heart, as working for the Lord, not for men" (Colossians 3:23). This is exactly the attitude you should have in your second chair role, but you should also be willing for the Lord to move you to another place where you can continue to give your best to Him.

Leave as a Better Leader

Perhaps you have advance warning that a transition is on the horizon. You may know that you will leave at the end of an interim period, or you can see that the key role you have played will not be needed in the future. It is tempting to coast in this situation, but this is really an opportunity to continue growing as a leader.

If you are committed to personal and spiritual growth, you will leave as a better leader. Make the decision to continue learning and growing for as long as you are in the second chair. You might find this is a time to try something new. Have you had ideas for improving the organization that you never had the time or freedom to initiate? Maybe it was something you were unwilling to attempt because of fear of failure, but now the pressure is off. Is there a particular aspect of your leadership you have wanted to focus on and improve? This could be a time when you can ask more freely for feedback from those in the organization, and in doing so learn more about your own strengths and weaknesses. Perhaps you will discover specific training or learning opportunities—a book, or a seminar, or a course—that will add to your leadership toolkit. Perhaps the area of greatest development will be in your spiritual life. You will have more time with the Lord as you seek to walk with him through a period of uncertainty and transition. In other words, make sure you are leaving as a better leader, a better servant, and as a more mature Christ follower than when you started.

Leave a Legacy

This may sound a little arrogant, but you should make the most of your time wherever God places you. We mean that the organization should be stronger as you leave than when you arrived. If you begin to think about what the ministry should look like after you leave, you will be more attentive to what is actually happening from the beginning.

When Judy Shelley was hired as director of finance and administration at West University Baptist, our explicit goal was to upgrade the position. Previously, a bookkeeper was the only financial person on our staff. We knew our systems and processes needed a major overhaul, particularly in light of the growth of the church and advances in technology. Her husband's job transfer forced Judy to leave after only two years. But at her farewell luncheon, one comment was heard repeatedly: "I don't know how we could have gotten to this point without Judy." In her own quiet, behind-the-scenes way, Judy left a significant legacy.

To leave a legacy, you also have to develop others. If you do not, it will be difficult for the ministry to maintain its momentum in your absence. In *Good to Great,* Jim Collins found that the best leaders set up their organization for ongoing success even after they stepped away. Lesser leaders created organizations that were dependent on them, and they took a certain amount of satisfaction when the company struggled after their departure (Collins, 2001). Robin Smith says it clearly: "The church needs leaders who desire to leave a legacy." This is not a shrine to a leader's past accomplishments, but an organization that is healthier for the future because of his or her service.

You might even be able to leave a legacy yet stay within the organization. To do this, find a way to replace yourself by growing beyond your job. If you look deep and wide and begin to influence the entire organization through your relationships, the church may find a way to move you out of a particular ministry and into a new, challenging role. If this happens, you could have the privilege of hiring your replacement. In this scenario, part of your legacy is giving the newcomer room to lead so that he or she can take what you were doing to a whole new level.

Ronny Barner left a legacy in his music ministry at West University. During the interim after his retirement, several gifted lay musicians filled the gap. One of the strongest programs of his ministry was the church's youth choir, the WUB Singers. Several former members of the choir pursued vocations in Christian music or became key lay leaders in their church. Two of these former students, Hardy Fairbanks and Liana King, married each other and served as music leaders in a church in Indonesia while stationed there for a corporate transfer. They returned to Houston shortly before Ronny's retirement and were asked to take over the leadership of the WUB Singers. Ronny's legacy can be seen today in a youth choir that is strong and vibrant and that is led by two of his former students.

Don't Set the Bridges Ablaze

It should go without saying, but don't burn your bridges. Even if you are enduring great struggle, turmoil, or controversy, do not damage the relationships and organization that you have worked so hard to build. This is quite practical advice for the future of your career, and it is biblical advice for the sake of the Kingdom. If you doubt this, reread Ephesians 4:29: "Do not let any unwholesome talk come out of your mouths, but only what is helpful for building others up, according to their needs, that it may benefit those who listen."

If you feel unfairly treated, underappreciated for your unfailing efforts, or even personally attacked, your instinctive reaction might be to lash out. Even beyond this immediate response, you may feel justified in setting the record straight or righting the wrong (as you might see it) that has been done to you. This may feel like the right thing to do, but it is not. This response is likely to lead to further conflict that accomplishes nothing in the end.

We have both had experiences in which we left churches that we loved. Mike, in particular, was a deacon and highly involved lay leader in a former church. Over a four-year period after a transition in first chair leaders, Mike and his wife, Bonnie, sensed a growing gap between their dreams and those of the senior pastor. After a season of intense prayer, they felt that God was clearly leading them to leave. As influential lay leaders, they could have tried to rally the troops and fight for the vision to which they felt called. But Mike and Bonnie believed it was best to keep the bridges intact and step away quietly and without disruption. Many people pressed for more explanation of the departure, and some inappropriate and inaccurate things were said behind Mike and Bonnie's backs. It was not easy to leave, and it was even harder to remain quiet, but ultimately this seemed to be the wisest and most God-honoring decision to make.

Bridges, once burned, are rarely rebuilt. If your time in the second chair has been difficult, angry words may be on the tip of your tongue as you prepare to leave. Swallow them. One careless conversation has the potential to do incalculable and unanticipated damage to the organization you are leaving, and to you. On the other hand, keeping those bridges intact can be a powerful way to launch your next season of ministry.

Bless and Be Blessed

In the final chapters of Genesis, the Old Testament ritual of the blessing was bestowed upon Joseph, his sons, and his brothers by his father, Jacob (Genesis 48 and 49). Blessings are an important part of leaving the second chair. The departing leader needs to be able to bless the organization, including the first chair. He or she should receive a blessing as well. If you have taken the other steps that we describe in this chapter, these blessings will be a natural outcome.

It is not easy to leave well, but it is important to do so whenever possible. If you maintain a long-term, Kingdom perspective, God's grace will be sufficient to guide you through the uncertainty of the transition. He will guide your words and actions so you can bless and be blessed as you go. Robin Smith seemed to be in an ideal job at Oak Hills Church when he felt that God was leading him to leave. When asked how he could step away from the prestige and potential of this position, he explained, "God has an otherworldly way of getting you to do what He wants you to do." Even though Robin had experienced some frustration in his time at Oak Hills, he was also determined to leave well. As he and the church prepared for his departure, he asked Senior Pastor Max Lucado, two other staff members, and the head elder to "hand me over" to the church that he was going to serve. Two of these men recorded a message on video, and the other two traveled to the new church for Robin's first Sunday. They all described "what we found Robin and Karen [his wife] to be," what the new church should expect of them, and how Oak Hills was different as a result of their ministry. Each person then gave a spoken blessing to Robin and Karen as they began their new ministry.

But the real significance of Robin's story of leaving well is what he did at his farewell reception with the Oak Hills staff and church family. He turned things around, telling the church what he had found them to be, describing how he and his family were better people through this season of ministry, and offering his blessing on them. Robin did more than just leave his bridges intact; he left on a strong note for himself and his church, and he did it in a way that was surely pleasing to God.

If we all leave this well when the time comes, our lives and the lives of those around us will be enriched, and God's Kingdom will be well served.

A WORD TO FIRST CHAIRS ON THE
CONTENTMENT-DREAMING PARADOX

AS A FIRST CHAIR LEADER, perhaps you are frustrated with a second chair leader who spends too much time at one end or the other of the contentment-dreaming continuum. You may think, "Here comes that dreamer again," because he rarely engages in the practical details of the ministry. He spends too much time thinking or talking about how things should or could be, and not enough time addressing the realities of how things are in the present. At the other end, you may have a second chair who is too content to the point of complacency. You may wish she had a few more dreams and showed the initiative to do something about them. Instead, she seems content to go through the motions each day with little direction or passion.

As we have described, the contentment-dreaming paradox produces an internal struggle in the hearts of second chair leaders. They are often tempted to give up on their dreams or express intense frustration at the lack of progress toward their aspirations. It is not easy to develop and maintain second chair leaders who live and lead effectively in this paradox. The starting point is the same question we have asked in the previous two "Word to First Chairs" sections: Are you ready and willing to develop true second chair leaders? Doing so requires you to make a genuine commitment to understand, foster, and release their dreams. It also requires clarity about your own dreams for the future of the organization.

Clarify Your Own Dreams

If second chairs are to thrive in the contentment-dreaming paradox, their commitment to a shared vision is essential. The starting point for a shared vision is for the first chair to be clear about the vision. What exciting dreams and plans has God planted in your heart?

In *Leading Congregational Change,* Mike and his coauthors defined vision as "a clear, shared, and compelling picture of the preferred future to which God is calling the congregation" (Herrington, Bonem, and Furr, 2000, p. 50). The *shared* aspect of vision is to be discussed shortly. For now, think about *clear* and *compelling.* If your own understanding of God's preferred future for your ministry cannot be clearly explained to others, it will never be shared. First chairs are not exempt from the struggle between dreaming and contentment. This tension can cause them to compromise the vision or offer a vague description. First chairs need to ask God to clarify and renew His vision for their own lives and for their organization. Kouzes and Posner state it this way: "Leaders *envision the future* by imagining exciting and ennobling possibilities. They dream of what might be, and they passionately believe that they can make a positive difference" (2004, p. 53). Second chair leaders are looking for their first chairs to communicate the vision in a way that demonstrates deep passion and commitment. If second chairs sense this enthusiasm, they are more prepared to commit to the vision themselves.

Listen at a Deeper Level

What are the communications like between you and the second chairs in your organization? It is not enough to communicate your vision to them; you need to listen as well. Do you know their dreams and the sources of discontent in their job? Life for a first chair leader is busy and stressful. There are always more demands than time to meet them. Just like a marriage in which the spouse always seems to get the time that is left over, the time for heart discussions with a second chair often gets squeezed out of a first chair's agenda. With the day's crisis demanding immediate action, a philosophical discussion about future dreams can wait.

If you want to encourage and support your second chairs in the tension between contentment and dreaming, you need to know their dreams. Kouzes and Posner say that "teaching a vision—and confirming that the vision is shared—isn't a one-way process; on the contrary, it's a process of engaging constituents in conversations about their lives, about their hopes and dreams" (1987, p. 124). What do your second chairs hope to experience in their career? How has God wired them? What unique gifts do they have? How do they describe their understanding of God's call in their life? If you know the answer to these questions, then you have obviously spent time listening to your second chair leaders. If not, this is a great place to start. If you are just beginning the process, do not rush it. If a conversation begins with "I've got a few minutes before my next appointment, so why don't you tell me all the dreams that God has placed in your heart?" you can be confident you will not learn anything meaningful.

You should also listen for causes of discontent in their ministry. In some cases, these frustrations are just part of the job. For example, we all have people who are difficult to deal with or tasks that are uninteresting. You might counsel them on how you handle these challenges without being dragged down. As you listen, however, you may learn about sources of discontentment that can be changed. Are they in a role that does not match well with their dreams? Do certain aspects of your management style trouble them? This does not oblige you to make changes, but it gives you a wealth of information. With this knowledge, you might improve your relationship with the second chair or find ways to improve their sense of fulfillment. Deep listening begins the process of encouraging and releasing the dreams of second chair leaders.

Make Room for a Shared Vision

In Chapter Nine, we described the meaning and importance of shared vision from a second chair perspective. But shared vision begins with a first chair's belief that this is possible and beneficial. Think about your reaction to Peter Senge's assessment: "When you look carefully you find that most 'visions' are one person's vision imposed on an organization. Such visions, at best, command compliance—not commitment. A shared vision is a vision that many people are truly committed to, because it reflects their own personal vision" (Senge, 1990, p. 206).

Senge then sharpens the point by describing the value of true commitment versus compliance: "There *is* a world of difference between compliance and commitment. The committed person brings an energy, passion, and excitement that cannot be generated if you are only compliant, even genuinely compliant. The committed person doesn't play by the 'rules of the game.' He is responsible for the game. . . . A group of people truly committed to a common vision is an awesome force. They can accomplish the seemingly impossible" (p. 221).

Simply stated, commitment is when a second chair describes the vision not as the first chair's but as "our vision." This reflects a common understanding and passion for the vision that God has placed in both their hearts.

If your reaction is, "I'd be glad for my second chairs to understand and commit to the vision I've discerned," then you miss the point. The only way to build deep commitment, to truly arrive at a shared vision, is to involve second chair leaders in the process. If you want to see enthusiastic, 110 percent engagement by your second chairs, allow room for them in developing the organization's vision: "Leaders *enlist others* in exciting possibilities by appealing to shared aspirations. They breathe life into ideal and unique images of the future and get others to see how their own dreams can be realized by embracing a common vision" (Kouzes and Posner, 2004, p. 53). This does not mean you relinquish your critical leadership role in the process. Rather, you ask for feedback and input from other key leaders. You paint in broad strokes and allow them to fill in some details. You ask if there are other elements that might need to be added. You show how their vision is consistent with your own. Opening the process to this kind of input involves uncertainty and risk, but the benefit of experiencing commitment to a shared vision makes it worthwhile.

Discern Between Contentment, Complacency, and Discouragement

How much fire do you see in the eyes of your second chair leaders? If you tend to avoid confrontation whenever possible, not seeing a fire may be a relief. If your second chair leaders lack fire, however, it may indicate that they have slipped from contentment into complacency or discouragement. Complacency is undesirable anywhere in the organization, but it is especially problematic when it appears in second chair leaders. If the fire is missing and you sense complacency creeping into their habits, it is important to assess the cause. Have they given up on their dreams? Do they think it is not possible for the organization to improve substantially? Do they feel their innovative ideas are always being shot down? Or have they just learned that they can get away with coasting?

If this last notion is true, it may be time for a serious motivational talk. But do not jump to this conclusion quickly. A true second chair leader is personally motivated and has a genuine desire for the organization to succeed. If complacency is the result of dying dreams, then a pep talk may only lead to more frustration. Your second chair might need to rediscover excitement in her chair by redreaming. You could be the person who comes alongside and helps with dream stewardship. Perhaps a simple pat on the back or a reminder of her importance in the ministry is necessary. Maybe she has pushed too hard and needs time to recharge her battery. As you interact with your key lieutenants, look into their eyes and heart often enough to know when and how to stoke that inner fire again.

Nurture and Release

A common practice in fishing is "catch and release." Any small fish that is caught is thrown back into the water so that it can continue to grow on its own. The opposite practice should be true for first chairs as they cultivate second chair leaders. The first chair's mind-set should be one of keeping and nurturing second chairs until they are ready to be released. Do all you can to help them become highly effective leaders for God's Kingdom, but know they will eventually leave. How do you know when that time has come? What is your role?

If a second chair is leaving because God has called him into another role and has released him from the current ministry, then you should release and bless him as well. This point of release can come for many reasons. Perhaps he is being called into a first chair role. Or the task God needed him to accomplish in your church is complete. It is possible the organization has outgrown him and it is time to make a change. We cannot possibly cover all the circumstances of leaving for the right reasons here. If the day comes, it will benefit your organization and you if you help your second chairs leave well. Celebrate their service, and send them on with the richest of blessings.

In some cases, first chairs cannot imagine releasing their second chairs. "We can't get the work done without this key leader" is not a good reason to hang on. God knows what you need before you even ask Him (Matthew 6:8), and He has placed unique parts together to form one body (1 Corinthians 12). Anytime He calls one leader away, He has a plan for how the ministry will continue. He is already preparing other leaders, whether inside the body or outside.

If now is not the time for release, what are you doing to nurture your second chair leaders? In one sense, this is the theme of all our "Word to First Chairs" sections. You should know the hearts and dreams of your second chair leaders. If you do, you are likely to be prepared when the time comes to release them. If you know their dreams, you will be able to maximize their contribution to the organization and maximize their contentment as well. If you know their hearts and they know yours, the subordinate-leader tensions will be minimized. They will know their boundaries and find the gaps where they can have the greatest impact. Our prayer is that your ministry will soar as you nurture second chair leaders to their full potential and release them in God's time to continue to serve His Kingdom.

EPILOGUE

THIS BOOK CAPTURES our understanding of the dynamic experience of leading from the second chair. Like you, we are committed to the local church. The church is the bride of Christ. She has great potential to change the world through the life-giving message of the cross of Jesus Christ. Since we believe this with all our heart, we are deeply committed to the leaders who serve Christ's bride. This work is not an exhaustive study of leadership, but we hope it begins a discussion that will grow and develop more effective church leaders. Our desire is to give you a new perspective on your role as a leader in the second chair. Actually, we have tried to establish a framework you can use to better understand your unique role from three perspectives.

The choice is yours. We introduced the three paradoxes with the analogy of a set of prescription trifocal lenses. Will you put them on? Some people who need to wear glasses refuse to do so because of pride or ignorance. We hope that nothing will stop you from developing to the fullness of your God-given potential as a leader.

Robert Quinn, in his insightful book *Deep Change,* challenges leaders who are not in the first chair to realize their potential to change the organization. He states that "a change in perspective can greatly alter how we see and relate to the world" (1996, p. 65). Quinn contends that "the problem is not 'out there' but inside each one of us" (p. 101). In his conclusion, he states that "we must accept the fact that we have the power and the ability to change. . . . One person can make a difference. One person can make a deep change in an organization" (pp. 217, 219). Quinn's words are an appropriate challenge and encouragement to all second chair leaders.

If you doubt your ability to make a difference, reflect one more time on the story of Joseph. A foreign slave with a criminal record became one of the greatest second chair leaders in history. God used him to save not one but two nations. At times, Joseph could do nothing to control his destiny other than remain faithful to God. This is the often-repeated pattern of God's grace and providence. Whether it is with a shepherd boy who becomes a king, a farmer turned prophet, a disgraced and rough-edged disciple, or an avowed enemy of Christianity, God chooses to do remarkable things through ordinary people. As a second chair leader, God can use you to make a difference.

It is not easy to grow accustomed to wearing glasses or to adjust to a new prescription. Just because it is difficult, however, does not mean you should give up. From personal experience, we know that the second chair leadership lenses are needed each and every day as you serve in your ministry. We hope you will wear them with pride and feel comfortable when you have them on. We trust they will help give you a clear perspective on your important role today, and that they will help you look ahead to your promising future. We pray that this simple framework might help you reach your God-given potential under the leadership of your God-given authority. The potential you possess and the authority under which you serve are both gifts from God, "who is able to do immeasurably more than all we ask or imagine, according to His power that is at work within us" (Ephesians 3:20). May God bless you in your journey of leading from the second chair.

THE PEOPLE BEHIND THE STORIES: PROFILES OF SECOND CHAIR LEADERS

Steve Ahlquist is the executive director of ministry resources at North Coast Church in the San Diego area (www.northcoastchurch.com), a church that has been a pioneer in video venues. He serves there with Senior Pastor Larry Osborne and Executive Pastor Charlie Bradshaw. In his role, Steve has responsibility for facilities, technology, human resources, and accounting. He is also overseeing the construction of North Coast's new 120,000 square foot facility. Steve recently moved into this role after spending thirty-one years as a second chair leader in the banking industry.

Tom Billings is the executive director of Union Baptist Association (UBA, www.ubahouston.org), the local judicatory of approximately five hundred Southern Baptist churches in the greater Houston area. Prior to this first chair role, Tom was a second chair leader at UBA, serving with then-Executive Director Jim Herrington. UBA is notable for its out-of-the-box approach to denominational work and its emphasis on team-based decision making. Before coming to UBA more than ten years ago, Tom served as the senior pastor of a church in South Carolina.

Kelli Caskey is the co-pastor of Crossroads Community Church in Houston (www.xroadsonline.net). Crossroads was planted in 1997 by Kelli and her husband, Guy. The church is characterized by its emphasis on global and local missions, a strong cell group infrastructure, and its desire to reach "hard core" unchurched people. Prior to founding Crossroads, Guy and Kelli served in second chair roles at the Fellowship of Champions.

Gary Ferbet serves at Memorial Drive Presbyterian Church in Houston (www.mdpc.org) as the executive pastor for program administration and outreach. He came to MDPC as the associate for pastoral care before being promoted by Senior Pastor Dave Peterson into his current position. In this role, Gary supervises all the pastoral staff and oversees the church's substantial giving through its outreach ministry. Prior to this, he served in five other churches, mostly in the Midwest, in both first and second chair roles.

Dena Harrison is the archdeacon and canon for ministry of the Episcopal Diocese of Texas (www.epicenter.org). She is the first archdeacon in seventy-five years in this diocese and reports directly to Bishop Don Wimberly. Dena has oversight for the seventy churches in the south region of the diocese, the ordination process, and the Program Group of the diocese. She is also the liaison for several of the diocesan institutions for which the bishop is the chair, including St. Luke's Episcopal Health System. Dena previously served the diocese as canon to the ordinary. She was the rector of two congregations and spent the first five years of her vocational ministry as an assistant rector.

Greg Hawkins has been the executive pastor of Willow Creek Community Church (www.willowcreek.org) since 1997, where he serves with Senior Pastor Bill Hybels. Greg's responsibilities include oversight of most of the staff, programming, and facilities. His career began in business with McKinsey and Company, one of the leading strategy consulting firms in the world. Greg joined the Willow Creek staff in 1991 as an intern in the small-group ministry. After facilitating a major strategic planning process for the church in 1994, he was asked to join the church's senior management team.

Ric Hodgin is the managing director of the A.D. Players (www.adplayers. org), a Christian theater organization in Houston, where he serves under the leadership of the founder and artistic director, Jeannette Clift George. Ric has been in this role for five years and has been with the Players for twenty-four years. His role requires great versatility, from acting to managing personnel to overseeing financials and other back-office functions.

Bob Johnson has recently returned to Chapelwood United Methodist Church (www.chapelwood.org) for a second tour of duty. He serves as executive pastor, supervising the pastoral and program staff and being the organizational person for Senior Pastor Jim Jackson. Bob previously served the same church for three years as minister of discipleship. In between these two assignments, he was the senior pastor of Mineola United Methodist in east Texas for more than seven years. Bob served as the sole pastor of two other churches and prior to that spent twelve years working as an engineer.

Dian Kidd is the associate director of Union Baptist Association in Houston (www.ubahouston.org), a position she has held during the tenures of two executive directors, Jim Herrington and Tom Billings. Dian supervises the consultant team at UBA and is a member of the director team. She is the person on staff who is known for taking care of the nuts and bolts and for having the flexibility to handle a variety of assignments. Dian has been with UBA for nearly fifteen years, beginning in an administrative role but quickly moving into a second chair position.

Kim Miller is the creative director of Ginghamsburg Church in Tipp City, Ohio (www.ginghamsburg.org), where she serves with Senior Pastor Mike Slaughter and Director of Ministries Sue Nilson Kibbey. Kim draws from her experience in theater and visual arts to lead the worship team in dynamically combining music, media, and message. She is also responsible for creative communications. When Kim came to Ginghamsburg ten years ago, she began using her gifts and passion to serve in a volunteer role. Within just a few years, she was in a full-time, vital second chair role that has helped to define Ginghamsburg. Kim is also the author of *Handbook for Multisensory Worship, Handbook for Multisensory Worship II,* and *Designing Worship: Creating and Integrating Powerful God Experiences.*

Preston Mitchell was a founding member of Fellowship Church (www. fellowshipchurch.com) in 1990. He worked as a volunteer leader until coming onto the staff as pastor of spiritual development in 1995. He was named the executive pastor in 2001 and serves with Senior Pastor Ed Young. He is responsible for advertising, communications, and public relations for Fellowship Church. Preston is also the executive director of Fellowship Connection, a network of eight hundred churches that share a desire to communicate the gospel creatively and compellingly.

Robert Moore has the distinction of serving as a second chair in Baptist and Lutheran congregations. Robert is currently the senior pastor of Christ the King Lutheran (Evangelical Lutheran Church in America) in Houston (www.ctkelc.org). He has been on the staff of this congregation for eleven years, the first five as associate pastor before he was selected for the first chair role upon his predecessor's retirement. In his second chair role, Robert was the only other clergy person on the staff and assumed a variety of responsibilities. Previously, he served as the associate pastor of Second Baptist Church in Lubbock, Texas.

Dan Reiland is the executive pastor of Crossroads Community Church in Lawrenceville, Georgia (www.crossroadsconnect.com), where he has served for four years with Senior Pastor Kevin Myers. He is well known as a coach to pastors and as the long-time second chair to John Maxwell at Skyline Church and Injoy, Inc. Dan is the author of *Shoulder to Shoulder* and other books, and leadership resources such as *Joshua's Men.* He also writes the free monthly e-newsletter "The Pastor's Coach," available at www.Injoy.com, and is frequently sought as a conference speaker and consultant to churches.

Warren Schuh has been the executive pastor of Calvary Community Church (www.calvarycc.org) in Westlake Village, California, for three years, where he serves with Senior Pastor Brad Johnson. At Calvary, Warren has responsibility for the staff, programming, and operations. He also led the church through a major transition when its former senior pastor retired. Before coming to Calvary, he spent four years as the director of Leadership Network's Large Church Network, a role that allowed him to interact with a number of first and second chair leaders. Warren also served as the executive pastor of Mission Hills Church in Littleton, Colorado, for ten years.

Glenn Smith is the director of New Church Initiatives, an organization focused on coaching and facilitating church planting movements (www.newchurchinitiatives.org). Previously, Glenn was the executive pastor of Sugar Creek Baptist Church (www.sugarcreek.net) for eight years, where he served with Senior Pastor Fenton Moorhead. In this role, Glenn was responsible for all of the church's staff, ministries, and operations. One of his major initiatives was a church planting effort that resulted in thirty-six new works. The spectrum includes suburban and ethnic congregations locally and foreign plants as far away as Russia. Before coming to Sugar Creek, Glenn was the senior pastor of a church plant and served in a second chair role in another congregation.

Robin Smith recently joined Farmers Branch Church of Christ in the Dallas area (www.thebranch.org) as worship minister. He serves there with Senior Minister Chris Seidman and Executive Minister Brent McCall. Prior to this role, Robin was the associate worship minister at Oak Hills Church in San Antonio (www.oakhillschurchsa.org) for more than three years, where he served with Senior Minister Max Lucado and Worship Minister Jeff Nelson. He also served in similar roles in two other churches. Robin is a gifted musician and worship leader who has a passion for leadership and for seeing the church reach its full redemptive potential in all aspects of ministry.

Geoff Surratt has been in Christian ministry for twenty years and at Seacoast Church (www.seacoast.org) in South Carolina for eight years. At Seacoast, Geoff's title is network pastor. He has responsibility for Seacoast's multisite strategy, which includes nine campuses with plans to grow to twenty or more. Even though Geoff serves at Seacoast with his brother, Senior Pastor Greg Surratt, he was not in a second chair role when he first arrived. His prior responsibilities included family, children, youth, and recovery ministries. Prior to Seacoast, Geoff served in one senior pastorate and in another associate staff role.

BIBLIOGRAPHY

Collins, J. C. *Good to Great: Why Some Companies Make the Leap—and Others Don't*. New York: HarperBusiness, 2001.

Collins, J. C., and Porras, J. I. *Built to Last: Successful Habits of Visionary Companies*. New York: HarperBusiness, 1994.

Covey, S. R. *The Seven Habits of Highly Effective People: Restoring the Character Ethic*. New York: Simon and Schuster, 1989.

Greenleaf, R. K. *Servant Leadership: A Journey into the Nature of Legitimate Power and Greatness*. New York: Paulist Press, 1977.

Herrington, J., Bonem, M., and Furr, J. H. *Leading Congregational Change: A Practical Guide for the Transformational Journey*. San Francisco: Jossey-Bass, 2000.

Hybels, B. *Courageous Leadership*. Grand Rapids, Mich.: Zondervan, 2002.

Katzenbach, J. R., and Smith, D. K. *The Wisdom of Teams: Creating the High-Performance Organization*. New York: HarperBusiness, 1993.

Kouzes, J. M., and Posner, B. Z. *The Leadership Challenge: How to Get Extraordinary Things Done in Organizations*. San Francisco: Jossey-Bass, 1987.

Kouzes, J. M., and Posner, B. Z. (eds.). *Christian Reflections on the Leadership Challenge*. San Francisco: Jossey-Bass, 2004.

Lawson, K. *How to Thrive in Associate Staff Ministry*. Herndon, Va.: Alban Institute, 2000.

Maxwell, J. C. "The 21 Irrefutable Laws of Leadership." (Audio album.) Nashville, Tenn.: Thomas Nelson, 1998a.

Maxwell, J. C. *The 21 Irrefutable Laws of Leadership: Follow Them and People Will Follow You*. Nashville, Tenn.: Thomas Nelson, 1998b.

Maxwell, J. C. *The 21 Most Powerful Minutes in a Leader's Day: Revitalize Your Spirit and Empower Your Leadership*. Nashville, Tenn.: Thomas Nelson, 2000.

Maxwell, J. C. *Your Roadmap for Success: You Can Get There from Here*. Nashville, Tenn.: Thomas Nelson, 2002.

Quinn, R. E. *Deep Change: Discovering the Leader Within*. San Francisco: Jossey-Bass, 1996.

Reiland, D. "Number Two: Called and Competent." *The Pastor's Coach: Equipping the Leaders of Today's Church*, Sept. 2002, 3(16).

Sanders, J. O. *Spiritual Leadership*. Chicago: Moody Press, 1980.

Senge, P. M. *The Fifth Discipline: The Art and Practice of the Learning Organization*. New York: Doubleday, 1990.

Stanley, A. *Visioneering: God's Blueprint for Developing and Maintaining Personal Vision*. Sisters, Ore.: Multnomah, 1999.

Stanley, A. "Challenging the Process." Speech presented at the Creative Church Conference, Grapevine, Texas, Jan. 25, 2002.

ACKNOWLEDGMENTS

IT HAS BEEN A PRIVILEGE to work on this project for the last several months, and much of our joy in doing so has come from the people who supported and encouraged us along the journey. We especially want to thank Barry Landrum, senior pastor of West University Baptist, who gave us the freedom to pursue this dream. But Barry did more than that; he helped us to develop as second chair leaders through his encouragement, empowerment, and example. He forgave us when we made mistakes, pushed us to grow in our faith and in our abilities, and helped us laugh and love in the good and difficult moments. We are truly blessed to have the opportunity to serve with such a dynamic and godly first chair leader.

Our primary learning lab has been our service at West University Baptist, and our colleagues on the staff also play an important role in our personal and organizational growth. Thanks to Ronny Barner, Barbara Chrisman, Charlotte Landrum, Lee Poquette, Judy Shelley, Kirby Trapolino, and Mat Yelvington for letting us use their stories. But more important, thank you for being the kind of colaborers with whom any second chair leader would choose to serve. Special thanks to Barbara for giving an editor's eye to the manuscript before the editor saw it.

The lay leaders and members of West University played just as important a role in this project. Several of them appear on the pages of this book, and many others taught and encouraged us along the way. With their faithful service, we are growing together to become more like the 1 Corinthians 12 description of the church: one body with many parts, each contributing to the work that God has given us.

The ideas in this book were enriched and expanded by a number of other second chair leaders who gave their time for interviews and their permission for us to tell their stories. Steve Ahlquist, Kelli Caskey, Gary Ferbet, Dena Harrison, Ric Hodgin, Bob Johnson, Dian Kidd, Kim Miller, Preston Mitchell, Robert Moore, Dan Reiland, Warren Schuh, Glenn Smith, and Geoff Surratt are real second chair leaders who face real challenges as they serve in a variety of ministry settings. Their candor about their successes, struggles, and lessons learned brings life and depth to the paradoxes of second chair leadership. Tom Billings, Greg Hawkins, and Robin Smith also shared their stories. But more than that, they provided valuable feedback on the manuscript and encouraged us by affirming the need for a resource such as this.

We have also been fortunate to have great support from Jossey-Bass and Leadership Network from the beginning stages of our work. Sheryl Fullerton and her colleagues gave us just the right mix of direction, reassurance, and correction as we navigated this process. Greg Ligon and Carol Childress believed in the concept from the beginning and gave us the guidance to shape it into a practical resource.

Of course, no undertaking like this is possible without a supportive family. Our wives, Julee Patterson and Bonnie Bonem, have given us the greatest gifts possible—time and encouragement—throughout this process. They are "helpmates" in the best sense of the word, and our lives are indescribably richer because of them. Some of the hours for writing were taken from time with our children: Brady and Cooper; and David, Matthew, Jonathan, and Hope. Each of them is precious to us, and we pray that every one of them will become the kind of godly leader that we describe in these pages.

Ultimately, our praise for this project must go to God and to Him alone. We pray with the psalmist, "May the words of my mouth and the meditation of my heart be pleasing in your sight, O Lord, my Rock and my Redeemer" (Psalm 19:14). Our church's vision statement ends with the Latin phrase *Soli Deo Gloria*, "to God alone be the glory." That is our invocation and our benediction.

ABOUT THE AUTHORS

MIKE BONEM has been a consultant and coach for churches, judicatories, and businesses for twenty years. He is the president of Kingdom Transformation Partners, which provides consulting services and leadership development forums for first and second chair leaders. He is the coauthor of *Leading Congregational Change: A Practical Guide for the Transformational Journey* and *Leading Congregational Change Workbook*. His work focuses primarily on leadership training, congregational assessment, vision discernment, and implementation planning. He obtained his M.B.A. degree, with distinction, from Harvard Business School in 1985, after having earned a B.S. degree in chemical engineering from Rice University in 1981. He began his career as a business strategy consultant with McKinsey and Company and worked with a variety of corporations and executives in the areas of strategic planning, organizational design, and change leadership.

Bonem is also a second chair leader at West University Baptist Church (www.wubc.org) in Houston, where he serves in the role of minister of discipleship. Prior to this, he served local churches in a variety of lay leadership roles. Mike and his wife, Bonnie, have been married for more than twenty years and have four children.

ROGER PATTERSON has been in vocational ministry for eleven years, serving as a student pastor for six years. He graduated from Houston Baptist University in 1995 with a degree in speech communication and Christianity and attended Southwestern Baptist Theological Seminary, where he received his Master's of Divinity in 1998. He is nearing completion of a Doctor of Ministry degree, also from Southwestern.

Patterson is a second chair leader, having served West University Baptist Church (www.wubc.org) for the past eight years, starting in the role of minister to students. He has been the associate pastor since January 1999 with a variety of duties, including staff and facility administration, strategic planning, construction management, and preaching and teaching responsibilities. Since January 2005, he has taken on additional responsibilities of preaching each week at one of the two campuses of West University Baptist Church.

He has been married to his wife, Julee, for ten years and they have two sons, Brady Jackson (four) and Cooper Grayson (one). He enjoys spending time with his family and playing golf.

Contact the authors for questions or to inquire about consulting or training services at

Kingdom Transformation Partners
www.secondchairleaders.com

INDEX